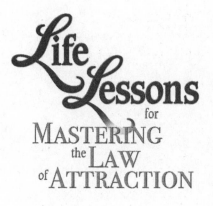

Life Lessons

for
MASTERING
the LAW
of ATTRACTION

Life Lessons for

MASTERING the LAW of ATTRACTION

7 Essential Ingredients for Living a Prosperous Life

Jack Canfield
Mark Victor Hansen
Jeanna Gabellini
Eva Gregory

Health Communications, Inc.
Deerfield Beach, Florida

www.hcibooks.com
www.chickensoup.com

We would like to acknowledge the many publishers and individuals who granted us permission to reprint the cited material. (Note: The stories that were written by Jack Canfield, Mark Victor Hansen, Jeanna Gabellini, or Eva Gregory are not included in this listing.)

Letting In the Slim. Reprinted by permission of Patricia Daniels. ©2007 Patricia Daniels.

Take Advantage of Opportunities. Reprinted by permission of Ruben Gonzalez. ©2004 Ruben Gonzalez.

Friends in France. ©2005 by Sonia Loraine Choquette. First published by Random House, Inc. Repritned by permission of the author and Susan Schulman, A Literary Agency, New York.

(Continued on page 329)

Library of Congress Cataloging-in-Publication Data

Life lessons for mastering the law of attraction : 7 essential ingredients to living a prosperous life / Jack Canfield . . . [et al.].
   p. cm.
   ISBN-13: 978-0-7573-0669-3 (trade paper)
   ISBN-10: 0-7573-0669-1 (trade paper)
   1. Success—Psychological aspects.   2. Intentionalism.   3. Health.
   4. Wealth.   I. Canfield, Jack, 1944-
   BF637.S8L4855 2008
   650.1—dc22

2007052681

Publisher: Health Communications, Inc.
          3201 S.W. 15th Street
          Deerfield Beach, FL 33442–8190

R-04-08

Cover graphic by Ronda Taylor
Cover design by Larissa Hise Henoch
Inside formatting by Dawn Von Strolley Grove

Contents

Acknowledgments ix

Introduction. xiii

Essential Ingredient #1: Here's How It Works

Life Lesson #1: Let Your Passion Be Your Guide 3

Letting In the Slim *Patricia Daniels* 4

Life Lesson #2: What You Think and What You Feel

    Are Always a Match 13

Take Advantage of Opportunities *Ruben Gonzalez* 14

Life Lesson #3: Releasing the "How" So the Dream Can Unfold . . 23

Friends in France *Sonia Choquette* 24

Life Lesson #4: The Power of Your State of Mind 31

Allow, and Prosperity Follows *Eva Gregory* 32

Life Lesson #5: The Power of Intention, Not Attachment 40

What Is Your Brown Rice? *Kristy Iris* 41

Essential Ingredient #2: Defining Moments

Life Lesson #1: You're Never Stuck! 49

From Rags to Faith and, Finally, to Riches! *Idelisa Cintron* 50

Life Lesson #2: Breakthroughs Don't Have to Be Hard 57

Kisses for Mr. Castle *Terri Elders, LCSW* 58

Life Lesson #3: Where You Currently Stand Is Perfect 67

The Day I Ran Out of Money *Amy Scott Grant* 68

Life Lesson #4: You Are Always at Choice......................78
A Gradual Awakening *Allison Sodha*.........................79
Life Lesson #5: Call In Your Team............................85
From a Bomb Shelter to the Beach House *Jim Bunch*..........86

Essential Ingredient #3: Transforming Thoughts

Life Lesson #1: Don't Take It Personally......................97
Attracting Harmony in Your Life *Randy Gage*.................98
Life Lesson #2: Where Thought Goes, Energy Flows..........106
I Love My Hair *Catherine Ripley Greene, D.C.*...................107
Life Lesson #3: Seeing the Glass Half-Full....................117
The Healing Power of Intention *Kathleen Carroll*.............118
Life Lesson #4: Letting Go to Let It Flow....................121
There Is Enough Money for Everyone *Carol Tuttle*...........122
Life Lesson #5: Empower Yourself for Success................131
Until You Value Yourself . . . Don't Expect
   Anyone Else To *Dr. John F. Demartini*.....................132

Essential Ingredient #4: Inspired Actions

Life Lesson #1: First Things First 141
The Journey of the Wanderin' Berrys *Licia Berry* 142
Life Lesson #2: The Time Is Now 149
Free Hugs *Christine Brooks*.................................150
Life Lesson #3: Stop, Look, and Listen 158
Prosperity Starts at the Kitchen Table *Jan Stringer*...........159
Life Lesson #4: Relax Awhile and Allow......................165
Goofing Off to Get Ahead *Jeannette Maw*.....................166
Life Lesson #5: Trust "The" Voice 173

How Two Dozen Eggs Hatched
  My Real-Estate Career *Holleay Parcker* 174

Essential Ingredient #5: Baby Steps Lead to Avalanches

Life Lesson #1: The Power of a Single Step 185
A Poor Village Boy's Journey to
  the American Dream *Rene Godefroy* 186
Life Lesson #2: The Power of Being 100 Percent Responsible .. 196
Success in the Face of Adversity *Charles Marcus* 197
Life Lesson #3: Pay It Forward and Create Miracles.......... 204
Dave's Legacy: The Miracle of Giving *Barb Gau, MSW, LCSW*.. 205
Life Lesson #4: How to Make Fear Your Ally 211
Somebody Give Me a Hand *Jeanna Gabellini* 212
Life Lesson #5: Close Your Eyes and Dream 218
Flash of Inspiration *Jillian Coleman Wheeler*. 219

Essential Ingredient #6: Your Full Potential

Life Lesson #1: Live Life Fully 229
Radical Sabbatical *Betty Healey, M.Ed.*...................... 230
Life Lesson #2: One Giant Leap for the Life You Love........ 237
It's Never Too Late to Pursue Your Destiny *Patrick Snow* 238
Life Lesson #3: If You Want It, You Can Have It.............. 244
Transforming Thoughts *Wanda Peyton* 245
Life Lesson #4: You've Got It All............................. 253
List for It *Hayley Foster*...................................... 254
Life Lesson #5: Your Wealth Depends on You................ 263
Shake That Money Tree *Jan Henrikson*...................... 264

Essential Ingredient #7: Acts of Faith

Life Lesson #1: The Secret to Making It B-I-G 273

What Is the Best Use of a Life
   Given This Much Good Fortune? *Dave Ellis* 274

Life Lesson #2: Givers Always Gain......................... 282

The Greatest Money-Making Secret in History *Joe Vitale* 283

Life Lesson #3: Your Intuition Knows 292

The Valentine's Day Cruise *Maureen O'Shaughnessy* 293

Life Lesson #4: Putting Actions to Your Intentions........... 299

My Dream House *Noelle Nelson* 300

Life Lesson #5: Inner Guidance Is Always with You.......... 308

A Leap of Faith! *Sharon Wilson*............................ 309

A Final Word 317

More Chicken Soup? 318

Supporting Others 319

Who Is Jack Canfield? 321

Who Is Mark Victor Hansen?.............................. 322

Who Is Jeanna Gabellini? 323

Who Is Eva Gregory?..................................... 324

Contributors 325

Permissions (*continued*)................................... 329

Acknowledgments

We want to convey our deepest gratitude to the following people who helped make this book possible.

From Jeanna: Thank you, Eva, for being my most perfect business partner and dearest friend. When the diva is inspired, look out! To my mom and dad, who think that whatever I decide to do is natural for me to make it happen. Thank you, Steve, for always telling me it's all going to work out. You're right—everything always works out. I deeply appreciate the Universe for delivering the best man, family, friends, clients, and coaches a girl could ask for.

From Eva: Thank you, Robin, for your love and support for the past twenty-four years. It continues to be the Law of Attraction and co-creation at its best. To my son, Jeffrey, and his wife, Kristine—you bring me great joy. To my precious grandbabies, Savannah and Drew—you fill my heart until I think it just might burst from so much love. And Jeanna, you have my heart!

Special acknowledgements of gratitude to Jeanna's and Eva's core team:

To our talented staff, we thank you for your support in keeping our sanity intact and our businesses and projects running smoothly: Lauray Walsh, Sarah Lateer, Ronda Taylor, Jon Kip, Nancy Tierney, and Kim Green-Spangler. You rock!

An additional thanks to Ronda Taylor for the killer cover design for our book. You read our minds!

To our favorite copy editor, Veronica Yates. Thank you for your commitment to the project in spite of our wild and crazy deadlines. We could not have done it without you. It's a good thing you love us!

To our Chicken Soup team members: D'ette Corona, who was our point person and fabulously supportive guide. You made our first Chicken Soup experience a delicious one. Patty Aubery and Russ Kamalski, for being there on the journey. Barbara Lomonaco, for your support in the process of identifying so many wonderful stories. Patty Hansen, for your thorough and competent handling of the legal and licensing aspects of the Chicken Soup for the Soul books. Veronica Romero, Lisa Williams, Teresa Collett, Robin Yerian, Jesse Ianniello, Lauren Edelstein, Lauren Bray, Patti Clement, Michelle Statti, Debbie Lefever, Connie Simoni, Karen Schoenfeld, Patti Coffey, Catalie Chen, Lauren Mastrodonato, Gina Rose Kimball, and Lindsay Schoenfeld, who support Jack's and Mark's businesses with skill and love.

To Mark Parisi and Lynn Resnick, for organizing and creating original and witty cartoons that get our points across delightfully.

To our gracious panel of readers who helped us make the final selections and offered invaluable suggestions on how to improve the book: Anne Nayer, Barb Gau, Bob Burnham, Charles Cassell, Dr. Cathy Ripley Greene, Delores Ziegler, Diane Case, Gail Crosby, Julie Sykes, Kimberly Hudson, Larry Guerrera, Linda Cassell, Mai Vu, Mair Hill, Marie Pippin, MaryBeth Rapisardo, Patti Garland, Rachel Anzalone, Rick O'Shields, Robin Gallant, Shelly Byrne, Terri Zwierzynski, Veronica Yates, and Wendy Young.

To Abraham-Hicks, Jerry and Esther Hicks—without your teachings this book would not exist.

To all of you who submitted your heartfelt stories for possible inclusion in this book. While we were not able to use everything you sent in, we deeply appreciate your letting us into your lives and sharing your experiences with us. We were truly inspired by all of your stories.

Because of the size of this project, we may have left out the names of some people who contributed along the way. If so, we are sorry, but please know that we really do appreciate you very much.

We are truly grateful and love you all!

Introduction

Did you know that the Law of Attraction works perfectly *every* time? It's a perfect match for wherever your focus is being held—whether knowingly or unknowingly. Focus on having a positive new attitude, and watch your mood lift and your actions match your desires. Think about your lousy day as you're drifting off to sleep at night, and your day may revisit you through your dreams, or your bad experiences could persist the next day, too.

The Law of Attraction is universal and ultra-powerful. It is like a magnet that is always at work. Basically, the Law of Attraction states that "like attracts like." In other words, wherever your attention goes, energy flows, and you attract more of that into your life—whether it is wanted or unwanted. In order to achieve the things that are truly desired, a positive frame of mind must be present.

Many begin practicing the Law of Attraction by making it a game—focusing on, or always finding a close parking space. When those things continuously show up (and they will), move on to bigger things. Just remember to keep it positive and keep your mind open to receive the things that are being requested.

Simply recognize where you are, where you want to be, and how you want to feel once you get there. Look at the positive future and forget the present reality—especially if it is less than ideal.

Like a conductor for a symphony, you can learn to orchestrate exactly what is desired for the ultimate life experience.

It is possible to be all, have all, and live all that is desired. It is possible to create the perfect situation for *you,* as the stories in this book reflect—personal stories of people from all walks of life who have successfully used the Law of Attraction to overcome challenges, struggles, and adversity, and to make their dreams come true.

The stories are organized within 7 Essential Ingredients for Mastering the Law of Attraction. They are intended to provide inspiration to you for achieving your own dreams, along with practical, concrete steps you can take right away to deliberately apply the Law of Attraction in your life.

The Law of Attraction does not impose limitations or make you conform, so don't limit yourself with your thoughts and beliefs. Revel in the freedom to pursue whatever your heart desires and be conscious that the Law of Attraction is always at work. It's simply your job to make it work in your favor. Dream on and dream big!

Essential Ingredient 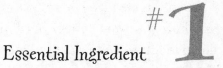 #1

HERE'S HOW IT WORKS

All the breaks you need in life wait within your imagination. Imagination is the workshop of your mind, capable of turning mind energy into accomplishment and wealth.

Napoleon Hill

Life Lesson #1
Let Your Passion Be Your Guide

··

We do not know who we are
until we see what we can do.

Martha Grimes

☕ Letting In the Slim

....

Believe in yourself, and you will be unstoppable.

EMILY GUAY

"Whoa," my friend said after seeing me for the first time in four months. "You are never going to be able to take off the weight you've put on, not with being in menopause."

I cringed. I usually gain a few pounds each winter, but this year I was over and above. I was unhappy with myself and my body, and afraid she was right. At the same time, I was determined to get back to my "normal" self, if possible.

For decades, I had watched family and friends struggle with their weight, going up and down like yo-yos, so I was not about to diet. I didn't know what to do—until I heard an Abraham-Hicks tape. Abraham said, "You cannot attract thin when you are feeling fat. Your work is to Let In the Slim."

Wow! What a fabulous idea, I thought. *And, yes, I am definitely feeling fat.* Right then and there I created a clear statement of what I wanted to attract. *I choose to be the perfect weight and shape for my body by the end of three months. I now release any and all excess weight and Let In the Slim.*

I repeat this intention before each meal and yoga practice. I rehearse *feeling* slim, walking slim, standing slim, and dressing to perfection in clothes that make me *feel* beautiful. I *feel* what it is like to be my perfect weight and shape.

I wake up at 5:30 AM and go for a two-and-one-half-mile walk in Central Park. Each day, I walk a bit longer, enjoying the smell of magnolia, apple, and cherry trees. I bask in the intense colors and scents, the raucous birdsong, and the changing reflection of light dappling merrily on the lakes and reservoir—the burgeoning sights and sounds of an abundant spring. I *feel* abundant here, as if I am in the center of a Monet painting, marveling at the explosion of green and blue, of frosted pink, and the myriad shades of purple and yellow all blending together, yet separate and distinct. I feel joyful, full of life and love.

I revel in the uninhibited, joyous antics of children— hearing their laughter, watching their intense focus on what is happening in the moment, while participating in their *Letting In*. I feel focused and abundant and happy on these walks. I feel good. I am *Letting In the Slim*. My fear is fading, and so are the *feelings* of fat.

Subtle changes are taking place in my body and in my eating habits. I eat healthily, but I also continue to enjoy culinary pleasures like wine and gelato, albeit smaller portions, savoring every mouthful. I play with a suggestion from one of the British World War II ministries to the public on rationing: "Butter your bread thinly and eat butter side down to the tongue for more flavor." Eureka! It works with everything I eat. And, of course, I reiterate before and after each meal that I am *Letting In the Slim*.

I want to have fun exercising so I create a ten-minute wake-up routine: abdominal exercises on the exercise ball, amped up with dance music. It is a blast and gets me feeling even better about myself and my trimmer body. I am now slimmer, trimmer, and healthier—I *feel* good. I am cooking!

Last week, I had occasion to wear an outfit I could not get into months earlier; it is now loose, and I look fabulous in it. On the day I wore it, a good-looking Frenchman unabashedly flirted with me, telling me I was very beautiful, and I *Let It In*.

Oh, yes, but there is more! There is so much more. Not only am I now *Letting In the Slim*, I am also *Letting In* more success and more money, new friends, and mentors to ease my way. An experiment that started as a fun way to lose weight has become a lifestyle, a pathway to joy and self-love as I allow myself to thrive and deliberately create the life I love. Letting In the Slim has opened the door to *Letting In the Love*.

Patricia Daniels

☕ LIFE LESSON #1:
LET YOUR PASSION BE YOUR GUIDE

Take a moment to think about who you are and who you wish to become. See yourself one year from today. If you could have anything you want and no possible way to fail, what would it be? What do you most want for yourself? When you look back on this period of your life, what do you want to remember? What experiences do you wish to have? What accomplishments?

....

Begin by getting a special journal or notebook, one that is beautiful and feels good to you. This will be your Prosperity Journal, which you will use as you read each story and go through the exercises in this book.

....

Exercise 1

Write a letter to yourself that describes where you will be one year from today based on the questions you've just answered. Date it and seal it in an envelope to be opened only by you, and put it in a place where you'll find it one year from today. Here are some ideas our clients have used to tuck their letters away in places they'd easily remember to retrieve them a year later:

- One placed the envelope in the bottom of her lingerie drawer with a notation on her online calendar one year out on where to look.
- Another kept hers in a "Bill Drawer" where it was visible all year and easy to remember to open the following year.
- One put his with the packed Christmas decorations so that when he brought them back out, he would find the envelope.
- One placed hers on the kitchen bulletin board where it stayed for a year.
- Several people mailed us their sealed letters in a self-addressed, stamped envelope that we mailed back at the end of the year.

The most important thing is to put it where you'll remember to find it a year from now. You can begin today. Design the life you *really* want—right here, right now!

Exercise 2

Start by looking back over your lifetime thus far. What things have you wanted to accomplish or experience? What is your definition of a great life? What is it you want to be, do, and have? What kind of life do you dream about having? What kind of life would give you goose bumps whenever you think about it? You can lay the foundation for it here and now. As you move through the lessons and exercises in this book, let your passions guide you. Look at what would be fulfilling to you or what would give you pleasure in life.

In your Prosperity Journal, write each goal, desire, or accomplishment you want to be, do, or have in your lifetime. Write each on a separate page. Write as quickly as the ideas come to you without analyzing, judging, or censoring what's coming to you. Fill up as many pages as possible. Include desires that may seem unattainable, silly, outrageous, or impossible. The key is *no censoring*. You want to get "outside the box" and expand your thinking. Following are examples of desires some individuals have identified:

- Drink sixty-four ounces of water a day
- Have my own radio talk show
- Spend more time in nature
- Take one week off a month to simply *be*
- Work three days a week
- Be the best mother ever
- Be debt-free
- Home school my son
- Own my six-million-dollar dream home
- Be a powerful communicator
- Take voice lessons and perform in the local theater
- Be physically fit
- Create a renewal/wellness center for new mothers
- Have my own housekeeper, landscaper, maintenance person, gourmet cook, and personal shopper

- Be a successful actor
- Establish a foundation for scholarships and men-toring underprivileged children
- Have a multimillion-dollar business that teaches people how to live prosperous lives easily and effortlessly
- Travel first class
- Be a full-time painter
- Be a successful keynote speaker on prosperity and abundance at $25,000 per keynote
- Be on the *Oprah Winfrey* show
- Take life less seriously
- Have fun in every moment
- Find the cure for AIDS
- Be a more loving person
- Own a home in California and a home in Sydney, Australia
- Be a successful writer
- Spend more time with my children
- Work out five days a week

Think about long-term and short-term desires. Identify desires you want to accomplish within the next week, month, and year. Now think out to five-plus years and write those down. Really stretch your imagination.

For additional fun and support, get a buddy to do this with you. Each of you can identify your own desires and then share them with each other.

As you go through this process, remember to go for desires that will make your heart race and give you those goose bumps when you think about them. How are you feeling right now? What thoughts are running through your mind? Perhaps you're thinking, *No way will I ever be able to have that desire,* or *Who am I kidding?* Give up questioning yourself. Get out of your head and into your heart!

If you're still having difficulty identifying your desires, put yourself in the following situation: You just found out you have inherited $1 million, $5 million, $10 million! (You name your number.) You are financially set for life and can embark on any activity, career, or project you choose. What would you be, do, or have the rest of your life? Spend at least five minutes writing out as many desires as you can, and as before, list each on a separate page of your Prosperity Journal.

How are you feeling right now? Have you identified enough wants and desires to say that if you accomplished these, you'd be living a life most people only dream about? If not, keep going. Exhaust all ideas and possibilities.

Life Lesson #2
What You Think and
What You Feel Are Always a Match

What is the difference between
an obstacle and an opportunity?
Our attitude toward it.
Every opportunity has a difficulty,
and every difficulty has an opportunity.

J. Sidlow Baxter

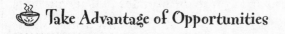 Take Advantage of Opportunities

We are all faced with a series of great opportunities brilliantly disguised as impossible situations.

CHUCK SWINDOLL

Opportunity is everywhere. Just keep your eyes open and focus on finding it. Once you spot an opportunity, if you decide you are willing to do whatever it takes, it's only a matter of time before you get what you want.

In November 1987, we had just arrived at the luge track in St. Moritz, Switzerland. We were about to begin training and qualifying for the World Cup race that weekend. The International Luge World Cup Circuit is like a traveling circus. Every week, you see the same group of athletes at a different track. We typically travel on Mondays; train and qualify Tuesday through Friday; race on the weekends; then travel to the next track.

As soon as we got to the St. Moritz track, I noticed something was different. There were only three sleds signed up in the doubles competition. Doubles luge is a wild sport consisting of two athletes lying on the same sled. They both steer, but only the top man can see. The top man gives body signals to the bottom man to tell him when to steer. It takes years to develop the trust, communication skills, and teamwork required to do well in doubles. I'd never done it—I'm a singles luge racer—but with only three sleds, what an opportunity!

I ran to my best luge buddy, Pablo Garcia of Spain, and excitedly told him, "This is our chance! We'll never have another opportunity like this. We have to find a doubles sled and race. If one of those other three sleds crashes, we'll have a World Cup medal!"

Pablo's no dummy. He saw the opportunity right away, but we still had to talk Coach into letting us race. We told him the opportunity was too good to pass up. It was even worth the risk of injury. Coach said, "If you can find a doubles sled in *this* town, you've got my blessing."

Finding a doubles sled in St. Moritz was going to be a real challenge. Even though they have a track, St. Moritz is not a big luge town. They love bobsled and skeleton (head-first luge), but hardly anyone in St. Moritz does the luge. That didn't matter to us. We were determined to do whatever it took to make it happen.

I spent two days knocking on doors all around town asking the locals if they had a doubles sled we could borrow. I was cold-calling in a foreign country—in a town that does not like lugers. They speak German in St. Moritz; I don't. But it didn't matter. When you want something bad enough, the facts don't count. You just do it. I knocked on the doors, regurgitated a German phrase I had memorized—*"Haben sie ein doppelsitzer rennrodeln schlitten fur die weltcup renn?"*—and hoped they would nod.

Eventually, I found a man who had a twenty-year-old rusted-out sled in his shed. He agreed to let us borrow it. We spent the next two days getting that antique sled race-ready.

On race day, everyone came out to see Pablo and I kill ourselves trying to do doubles. We almost did. We were on the verge of crashing the whole way down, but we finished the race. We placed fourth and actually received a World Cup medal. (We'd never even seen a fourth-place medal before; they usually only award medals to the top three finishers.) We got our pictures in the paper, and, best of all, we earned so many World Cup points for coming in fourth that, by season's end, we had a world ranking of fourteenth in the doubles!

The following week, the word that Pablo and I had taken fourth in the World Cup spread like wildfire in the luge circuit. Some of the athletes who had not shown up in St. Moritz heard about what we had done, but passed off our victory, saying, "They were lucky." Pablo and I explained to them, "Luck had nothing to do with it." We simply saw an opportunity and made a decision to do whatever it took to win. We made our own luck.

I guarantee if you develop that attitude—that you will go

for it and give it your all—your life will be a lot more fun. People will be amazed at the things you accomplish. Jump, and the net will appear. It really will!

Ruben Gonzalez

LIFE LESSON #2: WHAT YOU THINK AND WHAT YOU FEEL ARE ALWAYS A MATCH

Now that you've begun the process of identifying the life you really want, what thoughts come up for you? What questions are you having? What doubts are creeping in? This is about the time many of us tend to put up roadblocks to our dreams—usually without even being aware of what we're doing. The thoughts and beliefs we carry—usually unconsciously—hold us back from the opportunities that present themselves and from having what we want in life.

These thoughts might include:

- I'm scared.
- I don't know how.
- I've never been able to do this before. What makes this time so different?
- Who am I to think I can have everything I want in life?

- I need more money before I can have . . .
- What if I put money into this and it doesn't work out?
- What if I don't make it?
- What if I make a mistake?
- What if I waste all this time and effort and nothing happens?
- What if my partner doesn't approve?
- What if I fail?

Sound familiar?

Look back over your life up to now and think about all the opportunities or situations that didn't work out the way you wanted. Notice the areas in which you struggled, and then associate the thoughts and feelings that come up for you around those events. Are the thoughts and feelings positive or negative? Most likely, the thoughts and feelings are negative: fearful, sad, angry, frustrated, hopeless, upset, or simply resigned over what happened.

Now, think back over your life to opportunities that seemed to come easily to you, or times when you were happy. What were the thoughts and feelings associated with those times? You probably noticed it felt easy, effortless, exciting, fun, pleasant, joyful, loving, peaceful, natural, or maybe even just a non-issue! Maybe things went so well that you didn't even question why.

This all points to the universal Law of Attraction, like a magnet that is always at work. You will get more of whatever you focus on in your life, whether wanted or unwanted. Wherever your attention goes, energy flows, and you attract more of that into your life.

Look back over your life once again and notice the correlation between what you were thinking and feeling, and what you were getting in life. Now, look at your life today and notice the correlation between what you are thinking and feeling, and what you are getting in life. Are there areas in your life in which you are getting what you do not want? Have the dreams you've been dreaming up to now still not manifested? Are you noticing that they aren't here yet? Are you thinking it's really been hard up to now? If so, then how do you change all that in order to truly have what you want? How do you break through those barriers?

First, you begin by understanding that whatever you are focused on—and the emotional charge you have about it— is what you've been flowing to you. Think about this. There is no exception to this law anywhere in the Universe. *Absolutely none!* It is a law of physics.

Once you understand the Law of Attraction and its existence in your life, you can begin to deliberately and consciously change any limiting belief or limiting thought. The great news is that you *are* in control.

Seem simple enough? Well, it is.

Seem too good to be true? Hmm. Notice where you are putting your focus with that question. Flip it back around.

The fact is that it is simple! It is so simple that sometimes we have a difficult time getting our minds wrapped around it! The good news is that once we begin to play with this universal law and see it working in our lives, it becomes easier and easier to grasp.

Step One: Become aware of your limiting thoughts and beliefs as they come up.

Step Two: Deliberately change the thoughts from what you don't want to what you *do want*.

Example:

Don't Want mentality: My boyfriend left me. There are no men in this town. I'll never find anyone. I'll be an old maid.

Do Want mentality: He's not the only good man in this town. I've met several wonderful men. Someone is looking for me right now.

Exercise

1. In your Prosperity Journal, make a list of all the limiting beliefs and feelings you currently have around the desires you've identified. These are nothing more than habits of thinking you've had up to this point. That's all a habit is—thoughts you keep thinking over and over again.

   Examples:
   - My past choices have rarely been good choices.
   - It is difficult to find time to do what I need to do to achieve my goals.
   - I'm afraid of failure.

2. Now take those limiting beliefs and thoughts and deliberately replace them with a list of thoughts that support who you are, who you want to be, and what you want in your life. Go back to your Journal, and for each limiting belief you identified, list your new thoughts that support what you want.

Examples:

- To achieve my desires, all I have to do is deliberately focus on what I want.
- I am now willing to commit to the time necessary to attain my desires.
- I deserve to have everything I've ever wanted in life.
- Mistakes are learning opportunities to discover more clearly what I *do* want.

3. Understand that the limiting beliefs and thoughts you had may have stemmed from a positive intention. For instance:

Limiting belief: "Change is risky and should be avoided."

Positive intention: "Stay safe and secure."

Release the list of limiting beliefs you wrote down by:

1. burning your list of limiting beliefs
2. tearing up your list of limiting beliefs and throwing them away

3. _____

4. _____

You fill in the blanks. What works for you?

Life Lesson #3
Releasing the "How"
So the Dream Can Unfold

> When the truly great people discover
> they have been deceived by the signposts
> along the road of life, they
> just shift gears and keep going.
>
> *Nido Qubein*

Some people create their own opportunities;
others go where opportunities are the greatest;
others fail to recognize the opportunity
when they are faced with it.

WALTER P. CHRYSLER

All my life I had fantasized about going to the south of France, and these imaginings conjured up the most profoundly warm feelings deep within my soul. The more I imagined going there, the more I felt compelled to do it.

When I was a flight attendant, I met a fellow flight attendant who had lived in Aix-en-Provence during college. I told him of my dream, and he jotted down the name of the family he had lived with eight years earlier. He handed me that paper and said, "If you ever do go, call them and give my regards."

That piece of paper was a catalyst to my dream. The moment I received it, I decided I would simply have to go. I imagined renting a room in Aix from these people and living there for as long as I could. My images were intoxicating—lavender fields, *herbes-de-provence*, wine, cheese, baguettes.

I knew I had to go, but I didn't want to go alone. I

decided to convince my friend Heidi to come with me. By now, my imagination had completely taken over; I was forming plans.

"Heidi, come with me," I said. "I have friends we can stay with. It'll be a great experience!" I wasn't really lying. I had that piece of paper, and it *felt* very friendly.

I seduced Heidi with my imaginings, and with the assurance of "friends," it didn't take much to get her to go with me. I took a leave from my job, and two months later we were off. I had studied French in college and told Heidi I could speak it (although the truth was that I didn't speak it very well). It didn't matter. My imagination was filled with such lovely images of friends and fun that I felt what I knew was enough to get by. We packed our Sportsac suitcases and left with $500 apiece—a small fortune to us.

We were in a romantic, adventurous whirlwind until we hit Paris—expensive, impersonal, and overwhelming. We decided to leave after only one day.

"To the south, where the good life is!" we chanted, boarding the express train at the Gare de Lyon.

Halfway between Lyon and Marseilles, Heidi, now suffering serious culture shock and jet lag, asked me about my friends. Uh-oh. I was in trouble. I explained that I hadn't met them yet, but not to worry.

She was horrified.

Clinging to my imaginings the rest of the way, I moved

to the other side of the railroad car and looked up a cheap hotel in my Michelin guide. We arrived in Marseilles at midnight, and our taxi took us to the Hotel Martini, my one-star choice hotel. It was a seedy flophouse two blocks from the train station. Starving and grossed out by the hotel, we stuffed our money in our pockets and went looking for a place to eat.

Three blocks from the hotel, we happened upon a street fight between local drug dealers. We startled them, and they started chasing us, knives flashing. We ran screaming down the street, in fear for our lives.

As we raced around the corner back toward the hotel, a police paddy wagon shined its bright lights on us, and three cops jumped out of the wagon.

"*Arretez-vous!* (Stop!)" they shouted, guns pointing right at us.

We had only been in Marseilles thirty minutes, and already we had been mistaken for druggies or prostitutes and thrown into the back of a police paddy wagon! Not quite what I had imagined, but what an adventure. Heidi was in shock. I must have been, too, because I started laughing. The whole experience had become too weird for even my imagination.

Heidi demanded that I explain who we were, that we were lost and hungry and scared and . . .

"I can't," I finally admitted. "I don't know enough French!"

After a few more scary minutes, I managed to say, "We are lost!" in French. The cops conversed wildly, guns still pointed at us, eyes darting back and forth to us, to each other, and then . . . the guns went down.

In broken English, one policeman said, "Americans, no? You lost? Need a room? Yes?"

"Yes, yes!" we screamed. "*Oui, oui!*" Our heads bobbed like apples in a bucket of water.

He took pity on us. He bantered back and forth passionately with the three other cops for a few more minutes, and then said, "No worry. I help."

We were whisked to the safety of a beautiful country manor in Aix, our original destination! The policeman's grandmother fed us, and we were given a wonderful room overlooking a hillside of lavender, just as I had imagined.

"See, Heidi?" I said, finally drifting off to sleep in my cozy bed after our exhausting thirty-six-hour ordeal. "I told you we had friends in the south of France!"

Such good friends, in fact, that I ended up living there rent-free for six months!

Sonia Choquette

LIFE LESSON #3: RELEASING THE "HOW" SO THE DREAM CAN UNFOLD

If you've been following the lessons in order, by now you've identified your desires, both big and small. You've identified negative thoughts and feelings that come up around those goals, deliberately changed those thoughts to positive thoughts around your desires, and listed them in your Prosperity Journal. Great work!

Now notice if there is still a tendency to want to go to the *how*. "*How* am I going to make this happen?" "*How* can I possibly do this?" What do you notice happens when you go to the *how*? Does the goal or dream begin to feel impossible? Do you find yourself wanting to make the dream a little smaller so you can figure out *how*? Do you want to drop it completely since you can't see *how*? Is there a feeling of defeat or resignation? That's usually what happens when we try to figure out *how* we are going to achieve what we want in our lives.

By focusing on the *how* at this stage, you stop the process that moves you toward realizing your dreams. The *how* has you limited to figuring out a solution around what you know, rather than leaving it open to possibilities beyond your knowing. In going to the *how*, you are trying to *control* your future instead of *creating* your future.

You must be willing to forget about the *how*. Instead,

focus on *what, where, when,* and *who* around your goals. Never mind the *how.* The *how* will unfold naturally later.

The clearer you are about what you want and the more detailed you can make your vision, the more easily the *how* will show up for you. It's not your job to figure out the *how.* It's your job to hold the vision, the dream, the desires, and get as specific as you possibly can about what it looks like.

For instance, when you go into a restaurant, do you just ask them to bring you some food, or do you specify what you want? Of course, you specify. You look at the menu, and then answer more detailed questions from your waiter, such as, "Would you prefer that baked or broiled? Would you like a salad with that?" If you order the salad, don't you usually get asked, "What dressing would you like?"

The same specificity is needed for your dreams. The more specific you can get and still feel good, the better.

If, as you are getting more specific, you notice it doesn't feel good to be that specific, then back off just a little until you feel better about it. For example:

"I want to make $50,000 by the end of this year so I can focus on my art."

When you read a statement like that, how does it make you feel? If you feel a little constricted or find yourself trying to figure out *how* you would do that, then it may be necessary to ease up on the specifics and generalize more.

New example: "I want to find a way to be free to focus fully on my art this year."

How does that feel? If it feels better, then by all means keep the focus a little more general. Always remember, whenever you can, to be as specific as possible about your dream *while feeling good about it*.

Exercise

In your Journal, list all your dreams, goals, and desires. Expand on the desire by asking *what, when, where,* and *who* around each desire.

Once you've added the specifics, check in with your feelings around the desires now. Remember to release the *how*. Your focus is only on *what, when, where,* and *who*. Notice any negative or doubtful feelings that may come up, and then consciously and deliberately flip your thoughts around to thoughts that feel better.

Now ask yourself *why* you want each desire. Always look at what you *do want* versus what you *don't want*.

Life Lesson #4
The Power of Your State of Mind

Abundance is not something we acquire.
It is something we tune into.

Wayne Dyer

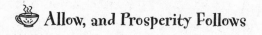

> *The people who get on in this world*
> *are the people who get up and look for*
> *the circumstances they want and,*
> *if they can't find them, make them.*
>
> GEORGE BERNARD SHAW

I knew the problem was bigger than me, so it followed that the solution was too. It was *huge*. Not in complexity, but in understanding.

My life partner, Robin, and I ran a software company in California, and it was leaking money like the proverbial sieve. For more than five years, we'd been searching for backing to help us launch the fantastic software program we'd patented—but to no avail. We were laying off staff, not paying ourselves in order to retain the crew, and morale was not just low, but nonexistent. Creditors were after us personally, as well as for the business. Our stress level was incredibly high.

I'd recently stumbled upon a universal principle called the Law of Attraction. Although I'd been studying metaphysics for years, as I found it extremely compelling, I only understood it intellectually. I really did not understand how to apply it to my life until I discovered the Abraham-Hicks website (www.Abraham-Hicks.com). I had a major *aha* moment. It was as though the light bulb came on, the fireworks went off, and I finally really got it!

Basically, the Law of Attraction states that whatever you are focused on you will get more of, whether wanted or not. But what I realized is that it is the *emotion*—the emotional charge you have on whatever you're focused on—that will magnetize to you more of the same. You can imagine where my focus had set up residence over the last five years: "We don't have enough funds." "We can't make the payroll." "We will lose the business." I had been focusing on exactly what I did *not* want more of in my life!

The engine of my thoughts was driven repeatedly by what was lacking in my life, and it was highly charged with negative emotion. I was carrying the emotional fuel that was magnetizing even more of what I did *not* want into my existence. And I had taken it to the ultimate level. Everyone within the company picked up on that vibration, and it grew to gargantuan proportions.

Once I grasped the principle, I felt I had nothing to lose by introducing the concept to the rest of the company. In order to change the vibe of the company by shifting our emotions, I created a company-wide game with a huge spreadsheet called the Prosperity Account, based on The Prosperity Game, a process I'd learned about through Abraham-Hicks Publications. We played this as a team.

The game went like this. On Day One, $10,000 was deposited into the account, and everyone in the company was asked to post to the spreadsheet how the funds would get spent. Each day the account was increased by an additional $1,000, so $11,000 was deposited on Day Two, $12,000 on Day Three, and so forth. After a bit, I was surprised to see how generous people were being. Since there was no fear of the funds dwindling, department members were making purchases for other departments besides their own. The money in our imaginary Prosperity Account was flowing, and we were actually having some *fun* for the first time in a long while. The goal of the game was to get our focus on something that felt better, something better than we'd been feeling for a very long time.

It worked. Overall, the company energy shifted, and many of us began to look forward to coming to work again.

What I've come to learn is that the Universe doesn't know if what we are focused on is real or imaginary. It only picks up on the essence of where we are focusing our energy and thoughts, and assumes it's real. So, as far as the Universe was concerned, prosperity *was* our reality. The Prosperity Account exercise showed me that no matter what I spent my money on within a given day, there would always be more in the account the next day. Therefore, I was able to stop thinking of lack and living in lack, as there was always an abundance of monetary flow. The exercise taught me to stretch my wealth mentality—a valuable lesson that must be learned in order to allow prosperity to follow.

And follow it I did. Within nine months of launching the Prosperity Account exercise, we were approached to sell the company—lock, stock, and barrel. We went from living from *no paycheck* to *no paycheck* (as Robin and I were not always collecting one for ourselves) to successfully selling the business for a hefty sum of money. Why? Because we were in a good place mentally, and we were able to see the opportunity for what it was and act on it!

Learning about the Law of Attraction and actually experiencing how it works was the most transformational turning point in my life. I learned that the difference between feeling hopeful and feeling fearful is the difference between success and failure. Fearfulness was not a good feeling. By using the Prosperity Account, I found a way to grab onto thoughts that made me feel better, which produced the key monumental shift. If one has to choose between feeling bad and feeling good, what is the logical choice? Seems a simple choice, though not necessarily easy, depending on your belief systems and where you've been focused over time. And yet, it *can* be both simple and easy. I just had to let go of my old way of doing things and embrace a new way.

Eva Gregory

LIFE LESSON #4:
THE POWER OF YOUR STATE OF MIND

Why do many people find it hard to believe there is enough abundance to go around? Many of us have been conditioned to believe that only a select few will reach the personal and financial goals to which they aspire. Or we have bought into the saying that "if something seems too good to be true, it is," and therefore we believe that abundance certainly seems too good to be true. In truth, abundance begins and ends with you—with your thoughts, your beliefs, and your actions. The abundance that shows up in your life, or the lack of it, is directly correlated to you and your beliefs.

Abundance is everywhere. Like Niagara Falls, it is a constant flow in its natural state, plentiful, only diminishing when tampered with. Abundance follows the same principle. It exists for everyone who keeps an open mind and does not diminish the flow. Besides Niagara Falls, can you think of another example of abundance? What about the air we breathe? Or the choices that are ours to make? Both of these abound.

If abundance seems to be missing in your life, what is your current state of mind? Are you addressing all of the things you would like to have but do not? If so, you are per-petuating lack and pushing abundance further from your reality.

Creating positive "I am" statements are affirmations of your belief in your power to be, do, or have whatever you say you want to experience in life.

Exercise

On index cards, create four to five "I am" statements to be repeated twice a day, just before going to sleep and getting out of bed each morning. Begin your affir-mations with *I am so happy and grateful that . . .*

Examples:

- I am so happy and grateful that money is mine to receive, invest, grow, and share.
- I am so happy and grateful that money flows to me easily and effortlessly.
- I am so happy and grateful that I am outrageously successful in everything I do.
- I am so happy and grateful that I embrace abun-dance, and abundance embraces me.

Your affirmations should not just be repeated, but said with belief and conviction. Do you feel power emanating from your statements? Do you believe them? If you are finding it difficult to accept them, give it time, but continue on with the exercise. It generally takes three to four weeks for a repetitive action to become a habit, and for a belief to gel. In time, the affirmations will become your reality, and you will find yourself recognizing abundance all around you.

Stop buying into the *not enough* principle. There is enough . . . more than enough for all of us. It may just take a little effort on your part to change your state of mind from lack to abundance. Don't you think you're worth it?

Reprinted by permission of Off the Mark and Mark Parisi. ©2001 Mark Parisi.

Life Lesson #5
The Power of Intention, Not Attachment

Great works are performed
not by strength, but perseverance.

Dr. Samuel Johnson

What Is Your Brown Rice?

*You don't give up the intention, and
you don't give up the desire.
You give up your attachment to the result.*

DEEPAK CHOPRA

I like sushi. Nay, I *love* sushi. On a cold, dreary day in April, I went to the market around the corner from me to get some sushi for lunch.

I looked at the offerings and asked the sushi chef, "Do you have sushi with brown rice?"

He looked at me, annoyed, and then barked, "No brown rice. White rice." Hmmm. He seemed a little cranky. I felt a challenge in that crankiness. There was something more. There was something stirring within me. I felt a deep call of service to help my newfound friend in finding joy in the lack of brown rice. There was some connection there.

I replied, "Okay, well, maybe tomorrow—brown rice."

He barked back, "No brown rice. White rice."

I shrugged, smiled, and replied, "Okay. One can hope, so maybe tomorrow, brown rice!" I bounced off, intrigued by where this was going. There was something deeper brewing.

A couple of days later, "Any brown rice? I mean today— brown rice?"

"No brown rice."

"Okay—maybe tomorrow—brown rice?"

As the cool spring breezes turned warm, could that be a smile cracking? "No brown rice."

"Okay, but just maybe tomorrow—brown rice."

And then, the next week, still: "No brown rice."

And the next week, we were well into June, and the flowers were blooming and a little laugh bloomed with the "No brown rice."

I laughed back, "Okay, well, tomorrow, brown rice." And I let my attachment to the brown rice go.

Our repartee went on through May and June and July. At one point, he took the time to explain that he has one rice pot to make the rice and just cannot make two kinds of rice. My response: I felt that I might not be the only one in my bohemian West Village neighborhood of New York City to like brown rice. I noticed a woman eavesdropping on our impassioned conversation. I immediately involved her in the debate and asked if she would like brown rice sushi. Suddenly engaged, she shyly nodded and slid off into the soda aisle. I looked at my buddy, smirked, and replied, "Tomorrow—maybe brown rice."

Finally, he laughed and shrugged. "No brown rice."

I laughed back and skipped off with my white rice sushi for lunch. I had no attachments to brown rice. Would I like it? Yes. Would I continue to buy my friend's white rice sushi? Yes, of course.

Then, in the relief of July's air conditioning, just as I was about to begin, "Do you have brown rice . . ." Wait! Yep, you guessed it—there, in all its beige glory, were trays of brown rice sushi! I jumped up and yelled, "Brown rice!" My friend looked at me with a sheepish grin and admitted, "Brown rice. Yesterday, first time for brown rice, and I sold out."

In the moment I saw the brown rice, I knew in every cell of my being that everything I desire, everything that *you* desire, is really as simple as the fixed attention of wanting brown rice wrapped around a piece of raw salmon and avocado, but with no attachment to the results. Focused unwavering desire can manifest anything. This was four months in the making—every week. And now, brown rice—the fulfillment of my desire, with better sales for my friend to boot!

What is your brown rice? What do you want? Speak of it, think of it, and then let it go. Let nature give you your brown rice. You deserve it!

Kristy Iris

LIFE LESSON #6:
THE POWER OF INTENTION, NOT ATTACHMENT

What do you do when you run up against obstacles as you pursue your dreams? You've come a long way to get where you are. And yet, when you look over the horizon, it may seem as if your dreams are still far away. This is *not* the time to give up! This is where your persistence can propel you forward. This is holding your fixed intention on your dream—but with no attachment to the outcome.

Rather than looking at how much further you may think you have to go to realize your dreams, turn around. Look at just how far you've come!

Although there are times when it makes sense to let go of something, often we make the mistake of letting go far too soon. A colleague of ours has a saying, "Just because the stew isn't boiling doesn't mean it isn't cooking."

If you find you've run into a brick wall with a goal or problem, or you have a complaint, turn the problem or complaint into either a question or a request of others, rather than giving up or quitting. For example:

Problem: "I'm too busy to focus on my dreams right now."
Question: "How can I carve out even a small amount of time each day or week to focus on my dreams and goals?"
Request: "I'd like to request thirty minutes of uninterrupted time each day to focus on my goals and dreams."

If you feel you've run out of steam around a particular goal or dream, look at what's changed. Does it seem like you've been focused on this area for a while and still haven't seen results? Is the goal or dream clear? It may be you've bitten off more than you can chew at one time. What if you chunked it down into smaller bite-size pieces?

If you've been playing with a particular goal or dream for a while, perhaps you just need to take a break. Release the attachment to having the dream for the moment.

A chiropractor wanted to increase her chiropractic business by thirty new clients a month. As she began identifying the steps to making this happen, she became overwhelmed with all the "Marketing 101" to-do's, and came to one of our sessions uninspired and ready to call it quits.

We challenged her to not only take a break from the process, but to take a break from the business completely! That takes courage. Her only responsibility was a week off to nurture herself and do only what she was inspired to do: play on the beach, go to a spa or a movie, hang out with good friends, and anything else she felt moved to do.

This goes against the grain of what we have been raised to do. Here she was wanting to increase her business, and we were asking her to let go of it completely!

She rose to the occasion and took the week off. Before our next session, she called to say she'd gotten some great ideas about how to put a system in place with the help of an assistant. The new system would not cost much. Within one month, she was getting her thirty new clients and they arrived over the Christmas holiday season, when her business was normally slow.

Instead of giving up, she released her attachment to the outcome, and while taking a much-needed break, held to her intention of a thriving practice. By doing this, the inspired ideas and actions came that led her to throwing out many of the goals and action items she'd previously assumed she'd need to do in order to be successful.

Exercise

1. In your Prosperity Journal, identify a goal or dream in which you've run into an obstacle.
2. Determine if the dream or goal needs to be chunked down further.
3. Turn the obstacle into a question and/or a request that would move you forward.
4. Review your dreams and goals and ask yourself, "Which dream or goal am I now inspired to focus on?" and work with that one for a while.
5. Acknowledge yourself for the progress and the changes you have made in your life thus far and celebrate!

Essential Ingredient 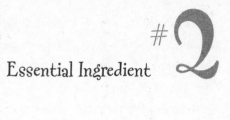 #2

DEFINING MOMENTS

I have learned that success is to be measured
not so much by the position that one has
reached in life as by the obstacles which he
has overcome while trying to succeed.

Booker T. Washington

Life Lesson #1
You're Never Stuck!

Burnout doesn't occur
because we're solving problems;
it occurs because we've been trying
to solve the same problems over and over.
The problem named is the problem solved.
Identify and confront the
real problems in your path.

Susan Scott

☕ From Rags to Faith and, Finally, to Riches!

*It is your responsibility to see
that your life works out the way
you want it to. No one else can do it for you.
The power to change your life is within you.*

HEIDI BAER

We had been living in a rented home for five years after my divorce from my first husband. We had two teenagers and one toddler. Our master bedroom was a bedroom for us, a bed for the little one, and an office—all in one.

I'd had a great life financially with my prior husband, but I hadn't been happy.

After the divorce, I received a nice settlement and a home, but in my emotional state I sold the home, spent some of the money, and invested the proceeds of almost $120,000 with a person I trusted completely.

Everything seemed fine for a year—I was getting interest checks and really thought I had made a good decision—but eventually those checks started to be returned unpaid, and then the excuses started. The government was freezing accounts because of 9/11, and the program was being changed to private members only. Investors were promised they would be able to withdraw their money, and everything would be fine.

By then, I had remarried. My husband and I wavered from hope to despair in a matter of seconds; we didn't know what to believe. Even with all of the excuses, I still believed this woman with whom I had invested my money. The lies continued for two years.

Finally, we received a notice from the California Department of Corporation. They informed us that the investment firm was a fraudulent operation known as a Ponzi scheme, and that we had lost all of our money.

That money had been earmarked for a down payment on our future home and college money for my kids. We lost it all, and we were barely making it month to month. My heart and spirit were absolutely broken when I realized it was all gone. I had to take full responsibility for my horrible decision, and I began to lose hope. We also had to file bankruptcy. I really felt our financial lives were ruined. I asked myself, *How did I get so far off course?* We had to start all over again, and I was already in my early forties with two teenagers who were getting ready to go to college.

I had read *The Science of Getting Rich* many years ago, but I hadn't referred to it in a very long time. However, at that moment, I realized I had lost the future security of my family, and my only hope was to pick up that book again and apply its principles religiously. My spiritual quest began again with a vengeance.

I went deep within and read and listened to anything

and everything that would give me hope on a daily basis. I wrote intentions, made vision boards, and visualized everything I desired for my family and myself. I even started to take action and looked for homes that would provide us with a safe haven in a wonderful neighborhood, with great neighbors and lots of kids.

While my husband and I looked at our finances, all of the banks and brokers told us we would not be able to get the home we desired. They said we didn't make enough money and had a bankruptcy on record. But I wouldn't give up. I kept focused, and I kept looking for someone to help in both the spiritual and physical realm.

One day, I stumbled upon personal-development speaker Steve Pavlina's website and discovered the "Million Dollar Experiment." The premise was that we are all connected, and if we hold the same intention for the good of all concerned, then the intention will come true. I made the commitment and signed up for the experiment. I wrote down my intention and repeated it every chance I had.

Within twenty-four hours of making my commitment to the experiment, the miracle happened. My eighty-two-year-old father came to visit (I come from a poor family and had never asked them for money) and announced that he was going to give us $35,000! We were elated and finally felt the hope that we had lost for so long.

I started looking on Craig's List for homes that we might be able to afford. But again, real-estate agents and mortgage brokers told us that it was impossible for us to get a home big enough for all of us. I didn't give up and kept looking.

One evening, I checked Craig's List again and found an ad that was very different from any others I had seen. It read, "Own a million-dollar home for $4,500 a month." It sounded suspicious, but I was somewhat familiar with creative financing, and I decided to give the agent a call. We were very honest with him; we told him we had filed for bankruptcy and only had a small amount of money for a down payment. As it turned out, the owners of the home had purchased it as an investment, but the California market took a downward turn and the owners were ready to lose the house and their credit. The agent offered to partner with us. All we had to do was take over the loan through a trust, make a down payment of $25,000, and he would contribute the other portion of the mortgage. Because of our past experience, we consulted with an attorney, checked the background of the agent, and found that everything was legal and on the "up and up."

I am happy to announce that we are now in our million-dollar home with a room for everyone, an office for me, a neighborhood with twenty-four boys all under the age of seven for my four-year-old son to play with, and neighbors who are absolutely wonderful. All of this happened within thirty days of making the commitment to the "Million Dollar Experiment." This was truly a miracle!

Idelisa Cintron

LIFE LESSON #1: YOU'RE NEVER STUCK!

Is there an area in your life in which you feel stuck? Maybe the word stuck is an understatement. Okay, the problem has been keeping you up at night for way too long, and it just won't go away. You feel helpless. You can't see your way out of the mess. Every solution you can think of seems like it has a big downside. The concept of win-win looks like some ridiculous fairy tale. Okay, enough of the doom and gloom already.

The reality is that when you feel stuck, it's horrible. You may have even tried dozens of times to create a different scenario, but still there's no happy ending. Many of us have "been there, done that," and don't ever want to go back.

Are you truly tired of your issue? How willing are you to take it on in a whole new way and stay committed to the process until you get your desired outcome? If you're at the point where you feel like, *I'm mad as heck and I'm not going to take it anymore!* then you're ready.

Here's a little secret you need to know: You're *never* stuck. It is your perception of the issue that has you either moving forward or running in place. This observation alone will increase your confidence about moving into the realm of hope. If you can accept this observation, you *will* feel better.

No matter where you are in any given moment, you *can* turn things around. You could be living out of your car and hear a voice way back in the depths of your mind that says, "What if it's possible to change my life or this situation?" This moment can be the turning point for you. You don't have to figure out the exact way you will climb out of the hole yet. You simply have to be open to the change.

Exercise

Is there an area of your life that you're tired of? Define it in writing, using your Prosperity Journal. Maybe someone has been pushing your hot button. It's time to *name the issue* and decide if you're ready to have it be different. Ask yourself what's really eating at you. In your Prosperity Journal, list any circumstances, people, and things that are causing you ongoing stress. Do your best to name the real problem, not merely the side effects. For example:

Side effect: *I'm overwhelmed, I have too many people e-mailing me, and I can't handle them all. Even when I'm with my family, I'm stressing about all the work and e-mails in my inbox rather than enjoying them.*

Real problem: *The lack of structure with my schedule has me feeling overwhelmed. I'm reacting to the outside circumstances versus designing a schedule and structure that works for me.*

Next to each problem you listed in your Prosperity Journal, describe your ideal outcome for each issue. *Ideal* means that every part of the outcome feels good to you.

Now it's time to make a conscious decision about each issue. Are you ready to have each of these be different? You're not figuring out how to solve the issue at this moment. You are simply choosing where to say "yes" or "no" in your life. It is absolutely okay if you are not ready to move forward on some or all of your issues. You are empowering yourself simply by making a choice, rather than experiencing something by default.

Life Lesson #2
Breakthroughs Don't Have to Be Hard

At any moment, I could start
being a better person . . .
But which moment should I choose?

Ashleigh Brilliant

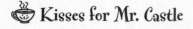 Kisses for Mr. Castle

"Give me a kiss to build a dream on, and
my imagination will thrive upon that kiss."

LOUIS ARMSTRONG

By eighth grade, at age twelve, I'd pretty much bought into the common credo that girls couldn't succeed at math or science. I still have my junior-high report cards to prove it, with those dismal Cs in science and math.

Even my parents reinforced the myth that girls could not grasp the subtleties of algebra or geometry, or succeed in scientific endeavors. In early 1950, we'd received a letter suggesting that my scores on the Iowa Standardized Tests were high enough to qualify me for a career in engineering. "It's a mistake," my father said, tossing the letter into the wastebasket. "They must have thought you were a Terry, a boy."

By the last semester of eighth grade, though, I had a goal. My English teacher, Miss Laird, had written in my autograph book: "Good, better, best. Never let it rest, 'til your good is better, and your better is best." Since then I'd longed for a straight-A report card to please her. But how could I get an A in my mandatory science class? And that year I had Mr. Castle, whose formidable science projects were well known.

We had to conduct research, prepare a visual exhibit, and give an oral report. Although we could be creative in choosing a topic, it had to relate to science. Science to me meant engines! Test tubes! Electricity! I still viewed the new television sets I saw in store windows with awe. To me, they were pure magic. And my father, a mechanic, sighed as he wiped his greasy hands after trying to interest me in how our sedan's motor worked.

"Some students do chemical experiments," Mr. Castle suggested when the class asked for project examples. I envisioned explosions that would hurtle us through the windows, with no "drop drill" exercise to protect us from the impact.

"Some like botany, and have collected and categorized various leaves into scientific classifications," he added. I couldn't tell an oak from a maple, let alone a phylum from a species.

After class I stopped by his desk. "I don't know what to do," I said. "I get stage fright when I have to speak, and my parents say girls aren't good at science."

Mr. Castle raised his hand to stop me. "No! Anybody can be good at science," he said. "All you have to do is be curious. Curious! Just think of something that you love, and research that. No matter what it is, you'll find it's related to science. Forget the stage fright. If you love something, and it's evident, so will your audience."

Besides family and Miss Laird, what I loved most were acrobatics, baton twirling, and tap dance, but I couldn't see how I could relate any of that to science. I also loved reading Ray Bradbury, but that was science fiction, not science.

Then I thought of Hershey's Kisses in their glittery little silver wraps. Though I later learned that Kisses dated back to 1907, during my childhood they were no longer around, since foil had been rationed for the war effort. Kisses returned on the market just as I started junior high, and I was an immediate fan.

I doted on them, but nibbled them sparingly to avoid the dreaded zits from dotting my face. At midcentury, we still believed that chocolate caused pimples, but Kisses seemed safe, not as much chocolate as in a full-scale candy bar, but a bit more than in one of the chocolate chips my mom used for baking cookies.

I'd found something I loved and decided to take Mr. Castle's advice to research the Kisses. In pre-Internet days, research meant heading for the encyclopedias. Luckily, I had library science as an elective, so whenever I had a spare moment between shelving books, I read up on the history of chocolate, and how the Mayans and Aztecs extracted it from cacao beans. I learned the chemistry of chocolate, and that its principal alkaloid is similar in structure to caffeine, providing that little lift. I charted out details of how chemists and biologists over the years had worked to improve the quality of chocolate by breeding a better cacao bean.

For botany, I tracked chocolate from Kingdom Plantae to Species Cacao. For physiology, I outlined the nutritional content of chocolate, fats, sugars, carbohydrates, and proteins, and demonstrated how the body converts food into energy. Still needing color, I wrote to the company in Hershey, Pennsylvania, pleading for product information. They responded with posters and photographs that arrived just days before my presentation. I fashioned a portable bulletin board from an old cardboard box, and then did a mental review.

"Appeal to our senses," Miss Laird had stressed, teaching us about creative writing. I had the senses of sight and sound down, since I'd be talking. But what about taste, touch, and smell? The answer came immediately. I needed the Kisses themselves!

Three hours of babysitting would cover the cost of two bags, so I hustled next door to ask Mrs. Kimble if she needed a babysitter since she liked to go to the Saturday matinees. "*Cinderella* is playing up on Vermont," she frowned. "And the kids want to see that."

I jumped in fast. "Why don't I take Bobby and Biddy to *Cinderella*, and you can go to see *All About Eve* at the Arden?" I asked for a dollar to cover my admission and three hours of babysitting. That was just enough to buy two bags of Kisses so everybody in the class could have seconds.

"Bette Davis is my favorite," Mrs. Kimble agreed. "It's a deal."

The day of my presentation, I marched confidently into science class, tossing a smile toward Mr. Castle. After a lackluster procession of reports from others, I strode to the front of the class, unfurled my posters, and then propped up my bulletin board.

I dug a bag of Kisses from my purse and began passing them around while I explained the science of chocolate. Nobody heckled me with "Kissy," which had been my biggest fear. Instead, eyes remained glued to me as I produced the second bag. "Just taste them, smell them, feel the tin foil," I urged. "It's all science. You just need to be curious!" Mr. Castle looked away, choking back a chuckle.

I got the straight-A report card I had yearned for, and Miss Laird hugged me. My parents shook their heads and agreed that somehow a mistake must have been made with that A in science.

Though I did not pursue a career in chemistry or biology, I overcame my fear of science, public speaking, and even of math. My curiosity remains, and it has helped me in my work as a journalist and a social worker. I'm able to speak before groups without a trace of stage fright. I did a statistical analysis of data for my master's degree and do my own income taxes.

In January 2007, the United States Postal Service issued a Love and Kisses stamp to commemorate the 100th anniversary of the Hershey's Kiss just in time for Valentine's Day. I arrived at the post office early to buy a book of them. Even today, I never turn down a Hershey's Kiss. And to this day I attribute my unashamed curiosity, which has led me to the some of the most exotic ends of the Earth, to Mr. Castle.

Terri Elders, LCSW

LIFE LESSON #2:
BREAKTHROUGHS DON'T HAVE TO BE HARD

A simple shift in perception can create a life-defining moment. Being able to have a different spin on how you see yourself or a situation can open up possibilities you'd have not seen otherwise.

It is easy to make up a story about how hard a task, practice, or an accomplishment can be. Instead, what if you ask yourself, *How can I turn this around and make it fun?* Dramatic changes can be made in your life without the negative kind of drama that often comes with worry and frustration. Things don't have to get to the point of terror before you do something about them. You simply need to be willing to have the desire to shift your perception.

For example, if you thought it was too difficult, expensive, or time-consuming to get your private pilot's license, most likely you would never attempt it. You would cross it off your mental life-list of things to do. But let's imagine that a pilot offers you a ride in his plane over the San Francisco Bay in California. You accept the offer. It's a beautiful day with no turbulence. You have a bird's-eye view at 1,000 feet of the famous Golden Gate Bridge, Alcatraz Island, the skyscrapers, and Mount Tamalpais. The pilot tells you to take the stick and fly the plane. You do it with both a bit of fear and excitement. With some guidance from your co-pilot, you do a pretty good job for your five-minute debut as a pilot.

This experience has you questioning your prior thoughts about flying. Your Bay Area tour was addictive. You want more of it. You felt like you had wings. You contemplate the decision to get your pilot's license now. It's the experience that now drives your desire to make it real. You say "yes" to learning, and as you do, you feel more powerful.

In this example, the defining moment was getting the stick in your hand. It instantly changed the way you thought about flying. As a result, you are going to take different actions. You always had the ability to get the license, but you were focused on all the reasons it would be hard.

If you think something is hard, you will create evidence to be right about that opinion. The same logic applies to something you believe is easy. You will summon an abundance of proof that it is easy!

Life-defining moments can be stored in your mental data files for when you need them. These moments remind you about how powerful, intelligent, resourceful, and loved you are. From time to time, you may forget how amazing you already are. If this happens, simply go back to a life-defining moment and remember the time you went for that goal—even when everybody told you that you were nuts— and you nabbed the prize.

Your life-defining moments give you strength. They show you what you're truly made of. These lessons teach you which processes, practices, and people serve you well.

Think about the challenges in your past and how you met them. Think about how you got out of a jam. What were you thinking, and what did you do to solve the challenge? Whatever thoughts served you well back then may come in handy in the present.

Many times a defining moment is when you say "yes" or "no" to something to which you normally would have offered the opposite response—times you answered outside your usual response pattern. Have you said "no" to a relationship that lacked integrity and love, in spite of the courage it took? That's a powerful moment. Did you say "yes" to starting the business of your dreams or retiring, in spite of doubts or fears? That's another amazing moment. Even saying "yes" to tango lessons when you feel you have two left feet can be life-changing!

What you've learned about yourself and life from these defining moments can be used to make other areas of your life much more fulfilling. For example, if you've had a defining moment with your finances, you can use that same mindset to turn around your marital issues.

The experience may be different, but the three-step process is always the same: Decide what you want, give your attention to it in a way that feels good, and follow your inner guidance to take the steps that will be perfect for your journey.

Exercise

What are your life-defining moments? In your Prosperity Journal, write down at least ten things that turned your life toward a more fulfilling path. Look back through your life, appreciating all you've done, and feel the joy. Relive it, relish it, remember it as vividly as you can using all five senses.

Next, identify those thoughts and practices that served you in each instance. This information is your road map to achieving future desires.

Life Lesson #3
Where You Currently Stand Is Perfect

We do not see things as they are;
we see them as we are.

The Talmud

 The Day I Ran Out of Money

I've never been poor, only broke.
Being poor is a frame of mind.
Being broke is only a temporary situation.

MIKE TODD

I was thirty-one years old when I ran out of money.

Like many people, I had certainly been in a frighteningly "real" position at one time or another when I feared I would completely deplete all monetary resources. Fortunately, most people snap themselves out of it, or continue to live just on the edge. Not me. I managed to exhaust every single financial resource—every possible source of cash I could muster.

It was a nerve-wracking, gut-wrenching, emotionally defeating time.

My darling workaholic husband and I were both self-employed, but business was awful. We just couldn't seem to get it together, and we watched our bank account dwindle down to a frightening all-time low. We maxed out all our credit cards, and we were receiving more phone calls from debt collectors than from friends.

We asked to borrow money from everyone we knew. My parents had already loaned us $5,000, and that repayment was coming due soon, lurking over us like a dark cloud.

I had recently learned that my thoughts had created my reality, and that by simply changing my thoughts, I could change my entire world.

But I just couldn't help watching the amount in the checking account go down, down, down.

Negative thinking is a slippery slope. I didn't realize just how slippery it was until one fateful day when the unthinkable happened.

When I realized that we had maxed out all sources of loans, credit cards, and personal favors, and when there was just thirteen cents in the checking account and a mere seven dollars in cash between our two wallets, I gave up.

"Gave up" isn't exactly the right description—*surrendered* is more like it.

There was some canned food in the pantry. We wouldn't starve for at least another week. Seven dollars wasn't going to do much for us, so I convinced my husband that we should put all of it in the collection plate at church that Sunday. What the heck? It wasn't doing us any good.

To be completely honest, my motivation wasn't entirely "pure." The stress of the intense fear about running out of money was absolutely intolerable. I figured if I got rid of the last remaining seven dollars, I could stop postponing the inevitable and get this worst-case scenario over with.

The day we decided to hand over our remaining money,

I got dressed and found a twenty-dollar bill in the pocket of my jeans.

While I was slightly surprised and mildly amused, I maintained my belief that the situation was hopeless, and another twenty dollars wasn't going to make a dent in the mounting bills we couldn't repay. I decided to toss it into the collection basket as well.

That Sunday was a day I will remember for the rest of my life.

As I placed the last bits of my financial resources into that basket, I felt the most profound sense of *relief*.

Relief! I certainly did not see that coming.

Perhaps the most remarkable feeling was the sense that there was no longer a need to worry about running out of money—I had run out. Been there, done that, and can't afford the T-shirt.

And yet, I was still alive. I was still breathing. I was still married. My daughter was still smiling and laughing. We went home from church that day and cooked up a box of macaroni and cheese. That night, I slept better than I had in months.

Because of that, what happened that week shouldn't have come as a surprise, but it did.

Within the next four days, we attracted more than $10,000 into our lives. A friend spontaneously offered to loan us $4,000 to repay at our leisure—without interest. We owned a time-share we never used that was costing us money every year. If you've ever tried to re-sell a time-share, it's a bit like trying to sell a leaky bucket to the crew of a sinking ship. Ours sold online within days using free advertisement.

Over the next four months, we attracted more than $50,000 in new revenue. Sales were rushing in from our existing business, plus I created a zero-cost copywriting business out of thin air.

Within the next year, we generated more money than we had ever earned in a single year. Our existing businesses continued to thrive, and I learned to use Internet marketing to sell my own information products online. I was dumbfounded by the rush of success we enjoyed, and those info products I marketed online continue to bring in passive income.

The experience taught me many things, but one lesson remains clear: I am always taken care of.

I have come to believe that no matter what the circumstances may look like, our highest good is always being delivered. I am always being looked after, even when I'm doing my best to get in the way and muck up everything.

I had known intellectually that fear attracts what we do not want, but my experience of fearing that I would run out of money, and then actually running out of money, cemented the lesson forever in my mind.

I also learned that fearing something often causes a great deal more anxiety than actually experiencing the thing we fear most. I knew on an intellectual level that fear is simply "false expectations appearing real," but I didn't really understand the meaning to my core, the way I do now.

Since that "broke point," I refuse to allow fear or negative thinking to control me; I now know the price is too high to pay. Indulging in negative thinking for more than a few minutes can quickly turn into a few hours, and a few hours can turn into a whole day, which turns into a week, then a month, and next thing you know, you're completely broke, and you can't see any way out.

Now it is clear to me that had I been able to release the fear and shift into a sense of peace and freedom, I could have turned the financial situation around *before* I went flat broke.

Today, any time I am less than ecstatic about my financial situation, I can look back and remember that dark day when I ran out of money. I now see that prosperity is completely under my control. All it takes is one simple shift in thinking to create a massive transformation in my reality.

Amy Scott Grant

LIFE LESSON #3:
WHERE YOU CURRENTLY STAND IS PERFECT

Step one is to surrender. This does not mean you drag out the white flag, wave it over your head, and give up. Instead, you give in to the moment. You look around at the circumstances and embrace the situation. You accept it. You accept that you are where you are . . . for this moment. Not forever, just for now.

When you are up to your ears in muck, take a deep breath in through your nose and exhale through your mouth. Keep repeating this action deliberately. Then it's time to relax. Yes, it may seem like there is no way for you to relax with all the stress going on in your life, but relaxing and being present in the moment will assist you in thinking clearly. If you stop resisting, denying, or pushing against the problem, you'll find that your internal dialogue will slow down. When you are wrestling with life, it is exhausting. Call a timeout. Let in some thoughts that aren't bound up by the issue. Thoughts may sound like listening to a music CD that is skipping. All that is heard is the same verse over and over or fragments of the song.

When you breathe deeply and settle down long enough to be aware of what your body feels like, you're going in the right direction. Your body will tell you a lot about your mental and emotional state.

Are your shoulders pulled up to your ears? Is there pain

in your solar plexus? Maybe your jaw is tight and clenched. These are warning signals that your thoughts and actions have not been lining up with your desires and joy.

If you've spent a long period of time focusing on what is not working in your life, you may have taken on a chronic pain or illness. The body is your warning signal. It's saying, "You need to stop whatever you're doing and pay attention to how you feel. What do you want? What would feel better? What would you like to do next to take care of yourself?"

Now that you are accepting the current state of your life, breathing and being present to this moment, what next? Own it.

You're getting what you have because your attention has been on the problem and what's not working.

Taking responsibility for any and every situation in your life will give you your power back. You are the one who got yourself into these situations, either by default or not listening to your inner guidance (sometimes known as listening to your gut).

The great news is that you can turn any situation around, no matter how dark or deep. Things can be light and expansive again. Your job right now is simply to be present. You are at Point A, preparing to move ahead to Point B.

At first it may seem difficult to believe, but wherever you've landed in your journey is perfect. How can it be perfect if it feels so terrible? It just is. The things and people in your life that are presenting contrast to your desires are actually helping you to correct your course. They let you know that you're moving away from what you want rather than attracting what you want into your life. If there were no such thing as contrast, there would never be new desires.

Take technology, for example. Technology moves at lightning speed. A product is born, people use it, and then requests are made about how it can be improved. Improving a product doesn't mean that the original was a mistake or bad. How would we know what we liked if there weren't new products to compare against what we liked better or what we didn't like at all?

Your life is similar. Every choice you've made has led you to the next step. There are no right or wrong thoughts, feelings, or actions. The only thing that matters is that what you're focused on feels uplifting, joyful, or inspired. Negatively judging yourself about anything is like deliberately pouring lemon juice in an open wound. You're adding fire to something that already hurts. It serves no useful purpose, and it compounds the feeling of despair.

If you've tripped and landed on your knees in life, turn over and sit on your bum. Take as much time as you need to gather your thoughts and get connected to the stream of well-being. Then when you're ready to get up, do it with purpose. You may fall down again, but so what? It's all part of the process. There may be bumps in the road, but what matters is how you respond to them, not the fact that they are there.

Give yourself permission to be exactly where you are. Whatever the current state of your relationships, family, finances, health, or life balance, accept that you are fine.

Practice dropping the comparison game or self-criticism.

Exercise for: Life Lesson #3
Where you currently stand is perfect.

Here is a great way to be at peace with your life, even if you're not anywhere near living your dreams. Call to mind any areas of your life that you feel negative judgment about. It's easier if you write them down.

Do you have any constant negative judgment or guilt about your financial status? Debt?

Do you have any frustrations about your mate (or lack of one)? What about your family? Are you sick and tired of being sick and tired? Write down every nagging situation that you wish were different.

When you are done, choose one topic you would like to release. Imagine you can hold all the negative thoughts about this issue in your hand. You can begin to look at them from a different perspective. Take a nice deep breathe in. Continue to take deep breaths in through your nose and then releasing through your mouth. Imagine squashing all the thoughts into a ball the size of an orange.

Keep breathing. As you become more centered ask yourself some questions about the ball of thoughts you are holding. What is it made of? Is there a texture to it? Does it feel light or heavy? Does it have a color?

Decide what you would like to do with it. It's your ball of thoughts and you get to decide its fate. You can drop, burn, or dissolve it. You can shrink it to the size of a pinhead. You can throw it into the ocean. What about an imaginary laser beam breaking it up into dust? You can blow it into the wind. You can put it anywhere you want. Choose.

Good. How are you feeling about the issue now? Continue your breathing. Remember, you are bigger than *it*. These thoughts mean nothing about you. You can continue releasing the negative thoughts about the issue one by one.

Life Lesson #4
You Are Always at Choice

You always do what you want to do.
This is true with every act.
You may say that you had to
do something, or that you were forced to,
but actually whatever you do,
you do it by choice. Only you
have the power to choose for yourself.

W. Clement Stone

🍵 A Gradual Awakening

Freedom, then, lies only in our innate human
capacity to choose between different sorts of
bondage, bondage to desire and self-esteem, or
bondage to the light that lightens all our lives . . .

SRI MADHAVA ASHISH

Two years ago, I had dreams. I desired a happy marriage, financial freedom, a healthier body, and my own business. On the outside, it looked like I had a perfect life. I was twenty-four, married, lived in a beautiful condo, owned a nice car, and traveled extensively.

On the inside, I was crying for change. My marriage was dissolving. I was overweight. I hated my job and was in financial debt. For me, stating my imperfections out loud was unacceptable; it would have been expressing my failures. And I, Allison Marie, would never show my failures.

Ironically, I was taught just the opposite. My parents always encouraged me to express myself, find my path, and listen to my heart. My mother, a meditation instructor, would often discuss the process of creating our own reality. Since I was young, I often heard, "Where thought goes, energy flows." Even when I attended seminars with her at the Chopra Center, I believed the spiritual reality, but jumbled its meaning to fit my own agenda. I had all the ingredients for a blissful life, but instead made a deliciously unhealthy concoction.

And then I went to India. My friend Laurel and I were taking an eight-day tour of the Golden Triangle. It was only meant to be a vacation, but my life was forever changed.

It started as soon as we landed in Delhi. The airline had lost my luggage, and when we arrived at the hotel, we learned that there was no hotel room available.

Opportunity is often shrouded in misfortune.

Misfortune: Because we had no hotel room, Laurel and I were forced to wait in the hotel lobby for three hours until our room was ready. We were hungry, tired, and jet-lagged.

Opportunity: Parth was a travel associate who worked for the company that locally operated our tour. He kindly waited and conversed with us in the lobby until our room was ready at 5:00 AM.

We said good-bye that night. As I was in the elevator, I turned to Laurel and said, "I don't want to leave him." I found out later that as Parth was leaving the hotel, he turned to his associate and said, "I wish I didn't have to leave her."

Two days later in Agra, I vomited nine times in two hours, prompting Laurel to call a doctor. The diagnosis: food poisoning. It was completely surreal to be doubled over in a hotel room with a beautiful view of the Taj Mahal, an IV in my left arm, and a nurse holding my hair above the bucket. However, this moment of infirmity was also one of clarity. In addition to last night's dinner, I felt as if something else was being released from my system: my past. To this day, my mother concludes it was not tandoori chicken that caused my illness, but a release of emotional toxicity.

After Agra, my perceptions of reality changed. I woke up and screamed out loud about what I wanted my life to be. I wanted everything, and for the first time I *really* realized it was in my power to co-create with the Universe. And so I did.

I visualized everything: a joyful and passionate relationship, owning my own business, and getting out of debt. I visualized the happy Allison I used to be, the one hidden under my temporary identity. I also became proactive: I filed for divorce, moved across the country, and worked with my parents toward paying down my debts. It was the scariest and most fulfilling time of my life.

And then there was Parth.

After eighteen months of e-mails, daily phone calls, three more trips to India, and a proposal, Parth relocated from India to be with me. We were married in February 2007. He possesses every quality I was dreaming a partner could have, and his love is truly piercing and unconditional.

So, life does take form when you believe. I didn't realize

I was practicing the Law of Attraction until my family became obsessed with this little movie called *The Secret*. "Watch it," my mother said. "It will change your life."

And it did. Since my initial trip to India, I rediscovered unconditional love, started my own business, was published as a freelance journalist, became physically healthy, and am on my way toward financial freedom. The irony? None of it happened as I pictured it. But I believed in it, and that was enough.

Allison Sodha

LIFE LESSON #4:
YOU ARE ALWAYS AT CHOICE

Whatever area in life is challenging for you, only you can choose to make it different. Consciously and deliberately choosing an outcome is different from wanting it to be different.

There is a *big* difference between wanting, desiring, hoping, and wishing for a desire versus choosing and claiming the dream.

You must choose to put yourself in the driver's seat. If you want an ice cream, you must choose your flavors and place the order. Choosing is an action. It is an internal process that manifests itself through your attitude and actions. You can keep wanting your perfect house on the hill with the view of the water, or you can choose to have it now. If you choose it now, you will be very clear—it is yours! When you think a goal is possible, you will think differently and take different actions compared to when you decide you're stuck. You may feel inspired and call your real-estate agent. You tell the agent exactly what you want. You will not buy the house and simply settle. You choose the house you *really* want. You don't choose a house that you have to completely remodel in order to love it (unless you'd like that type of project). You *choose* a house you love.

Do not settle for anything less than what you really want. You are declaring your worthiness.

If you think something is not possible or is out of your reach, you're probably not going to commit much energy and resources to accomplishing that goal. When you decide a desire is possible and you're ready to have it, the Universe will assist you in having it unfold with ease.

Exercise

What are you choosing to claim for yourself today?

How do you want to feel?

Take five minutes to see this choice as a movie on the screen of your mind.

Close your eyes and take some deliberate breaths in and out to relax, allowing yourself to tap into your heart.

Imagine there is a twenty-foot-wide screen in front of you.

See the scene of your choice playing out in front of you. Listen to the sounds. Is there a conversation happening? With whom? What is the scene? Where is it taking place? Do you look happy and peaceful, or are you experiencing another emotion?

Step into the screen. Place yourself *in* the movie. Notice how you feel. Once you feel the scene becoming real, enjoy it. Take a few minutes to *be* there. Then close the scene.

Doing this type of visualization generates a lot of movement toward your desire. Even though you may not see it, you are literally amping up the vibration. This may be the most important action to take today toward fulfillment and joy.

Life Lesson #5
Call In Your Team

Interdependent people combine their own
efforts with the efforts of others to achieve
their greatest success.

Stephen Covey

☕ From a Bomb Shelter to the Beach House

Great moments await around every corner.

RICHARD M. DEVOS

For as long as I can remember, I've always wanted to help people be what they want to be, do what they want to do, and have what they really want to have in their lives. I've devoted my entire life to this. I've read books, learned systems, and given over 1,000 presentations with some of the most influential personal-development experts of our time. So, when my life crumbled to compost, I was deeply confused. How could this happen to *me*?

I had been living my dream, traveling the world, and changing lives for the better. But after a few years, something felt out of alignment. And the feeling grew. It was like a little itch, and it wouldn't go away.

When I finally stood still long enough to take a closer look, I saw that those lives I'd touched weren't really changing, at least not for long. Sure, people had wonderful realizations and found tremendous inspiration while they sat in my seminars . . . but when they went home to their families, back to their jobs and relationships, they went back to who they used to be. Our "life-changing" seminars weren't changing lives. And when I finally looked at that,

I was devastated. The meaning in my life just evaporated. Like water slipping through my fingers, my sense of purpose just disappeared. I lost faith in my foundational concept: that people can create a masterpiece with their life energy and become the person they always wanted to be. Without that piece, there was nothing left. That burning passion that had driven me for so long just vanished. Heartbroken and disillusioned, I quit my speaking job.

People talk of wanting to crawl in a hole and hide from the world, and that's exactly what I did. Because I had traveled the world for so many years, I didn't have a home to retreat to, and I had neglected my finances. I scraped together what money I could and rented the only place I could afford: an underground bunker beneath a stranger's house.

It literally was a bomb shelter—steep stairs descending into a dank room with no windows or natural light, and a tube to the surface for fresh air. It was dark, musty, and completely silent—the perfect place for someone so shell-shocked. I was disoriented, depressed, and completely lost. *What now?* I thought.

I had no job, no savings, and no way to pay off my growing credit-card debt. My family lived across the country, and my friends were scattered around the globe. For the first time in my life, I had no passion and no vision.

But even in that suffocating sea of darkness, there was still a tiny spark of purpose. In the depths of my despair, by the light of one dim bulb, I cracked open my copy of *Conversations with God*. And I sat there all night, reading it from cover to cover. The book reminded me that I did indeed have a purpose, even if I didn't understand the path to it. It reminded me that God was waiting for me to take the next step, and that he would help me find my way back. The time had come to turn the page in my own life.

Within the week, I had my pivotal breakthrough: I finally realized *why* these "life-changing" personal growth seminars were failing to change lives. People needed accountability and assistance to take a concept out of the seminar room and into their lives. They needed help to apply the concepts and integrate them into their lives.

And so did I. It was time to admit that I didn't know as much as I once thought I did, and that I didn't have to figure it out all by myself. For all that I had learned in my years of motivational speaking, I was the one who needed help to get moving in the right direction. Great things are never accomplished alone, and I finally felt I had something great to do.

So despite my dismal finances, I hired a spiritual coach to help me reconnect with my purpose and reconstruct my personal foundation. One of the first assignments he gave me was to dream about my ideal life. What did I want to create? From the place I was in, it felt so far away, but I could still picture myself living in a beach house, driving a gorgeous sports car, and reveling in the relationship of my dreams. And what kind of work did I want to be doing?

With time, I realized that I wasn't resurrecting my old passion; I was nurturing a new one. In addition to helping people change their lives, I wanted to transform our common model of personal development to one that works.

With this newfound clarity, I booked a flight to Washington, D.C., and walked into the Re/Max Metro 100 office. That day, I landed my first coaching client, and everything started to shift. The entire Universe stepped up to support my new path. After a torturous year in the dark, I built a six-figure coaching practice in ninety days.

A month later, I rented a condo on the bluff with a two-story wall of glass overlooking the crashing waves of the Pacific Ocean. I must have spent hours watching the dolphins, whales, and surfers 200 feet below. Getting the convertible Porsche and the relationship of my dreams took a little longer, but not much.

It's been ten years since I first descended into the darkness of the bomb shelter, and it was a rigorous transformation. Today, my life looks very different.

I've gone from six figures of debt to seven figures of wealth. I own several businesses that provide both passive and active income, but the one I'm most proud of is a coaching company with programs that generate lasting results for thousands of people, and provides rewarding work for coaches all across North America. My work has brought me into close collaboration with some of the world's best minds in personal development, and I spend several days a year with them to brainstorm human transformation. I used to study their books; now I call them colleagues.

And that relationship of my dreams? I'm living that, too. Michele is the most loving and supportive person in my life, and she just gave birth to our first child, Teagan. We snowboard together six weeks a year and vacation in the best resorts around the world. We've bought real estate across the country and built a solid financial foundation that will serve our family for years to come. I could not ask for a better partner, friend, and soul mate.

My external life is finally in perfect harmony with my internal aspirations, and I greet every day with the most profound gratitude. It's not the things in my life that I'm so grateful for . . . it's that resilient spark of purpose, and the helping hand that's always there. When you can touch those things, everything else is just a matter of time.

Jim Bunch

LIFE LESSON #5:
CALL IN YOUR TEAM

When you want things to change and you mean it, call in your team. We all have one. You may have several teams. You may have a team you use for business and another for spiritual matters or a team for fun. If you want an area of your life, or your whole life, to significantly change, it's a lot easier when you have support.

If the word "support" makes you cringe because you don't want anybody to think you're weak, think again. Robert Kiyosaki wrote a book called *The Cashflow Quadrant* in which he talks about why some people work hard and don't get ahead, and why others work less and have financial freedom. He demonstrates how most (not all) self-employed people are the hardest working quadrant because they do everything themselves. They enter a new business thinking it will lead to freedom, but instead it can feel like bondage.

On the other hand, truly successful business people and investors leverage people, time, and money. They use systems that will generate business and profit. A CEO has board meetings with her team to discuss new ideas and gets input from others. She delegates to other people and creates systems to make the flow easier.

If you only had your view and thoughts to use in life's journey, things would go painfully slow. When you want things to be easier, ask for assistance, tools, hugs, books, and whatever else you think would make it easier.

There are no awards for struggling. It is not noble. Put yourself in the presence of people who make you feel good and help keep your focus on what you desire. If someone commiserates about how bad things are, you will spiral down in their presence. Talking about what is giving you heartache is perfectly natural, but you will create more of the same if you stay on that track for too long.

Give more of your energy to what you *do* want and solutions that will keep you on purpose. Who on your team can support you in turning around your thinking and situation? Team members don't need to have the answers. They just need to assist you in keeping your eye on the ball and reminding you that you *will* hit the home run.

Team members keep you in the game. Even if you don't connect every day or every week, it's good to know they're cheering you on. There may be team members you get counsel from on specific strategies. Only use suggestions that resonate with your soul, no matter the circumstances.

You may know them personally or not. They can be friends, family, or colleagues. Some team members may be free of charge, while others you may choose to hire. They all serve their purpose.

Make sure you are using the right person for the position he or she is best suited for. If you're asking your mom for support on money strategies and she's up to her eyeballs in debt, she may not be the best choice.

When you are faced with something that feels much bigger than you, it may serve you best to enroll in a class, sign up for a retreat program, or get counsel. It's amazing what a fresh perspective can do for you.

In the event that you are working with people who have known you for years, keep personal history in mind. People you know well, however well-intentioned, may hold you as a victim because they know from your past conversations and actions exactly what you've been practicing. This is why objective team members are such valuable assets. They don't see you with all the old thoughts and actions in their vision of you.

When you are asking team members for what you need, be very clear and specific. When making a request, be sure they have replied with a "yes." You are redesigning your alliances in a new and powerful way. This new way of interacting may take practice for everyone involved. Some team members will give you exactly what you request, while others need reminding. It's up to you to get what you need.

Bring in the intention that the support you receive will be empowering and for the highest good. If a team member strikes out, will you kick him off the team? No! You keep seeing the team and yourself winning the game in your thoughts. This strategy works well in all relationships, whether there is a goal you're working toward together or you just want the best for them. Team players want to be there. It is their desire to assist you in attracting the outcome you want. It should feel good to both of you.

There may be former team members who no longer want to play your new game. That's great. Honor yourself and your team members by letting go and moving on.

Exercise

In your Prosperity Journal, answer the following questions:

- Who's on your team?
- What role do you want them to take on with you?
- How do you want them to support you?
- Are you forcing anyone to be on your team? If so, why?
- Who else could you find that's more suitable?

Essential Ingredient  #3

TRANSFORMING THOUGHTS

First comes thought; then organization
of that thought into ideas and plans; then
transformation of those plans into reality.
The beginning, as you will observe,
is in your imagination.

Napoleon Hill

Life Lesson #1
Don't Take It Personally

Attitude is the reflection of a person, and
our world mirrors our attitude.

Earl Nightingale

In this life, we will encounter hurts and trials
that we will not be able to change; we are just
going to have to allow them to change us.

RON LEE DAVIS

I woke up in the recovery room with the doctor hovering over my bed. He told me that they had had a hard time finding the bullet in my body, but they finally got it out. Then he casually mentioned that, as long as they were in there, they took out my appendix.

"What! Why would you do that?" I asked. "The gunshot wound is on the other side."

"Oh, it's just standard procedure," he replied. "Whenever we open anyone up for anything, we take it out as a precaution. That way you won't have problems later. You don't need it anyway."

I was incredulous. I simply couldn't imagine the arrogance and audacity of someone who thought they knew better than God what organs I needed in my body.

I left the hospital a few days later with a great deal of resentment. To make matters worse, the surgery didn't work out very well. The sutures came undone, and I looked down to see blood all over my shirt.

A week later, the wound became infected, requiring

another hospital visit. And the pain was unbearable. It didn't matter if I was lying down, sitting, or standing; I couldn't find a position that relieved the agony.

As the months wore on, instead of getting better, I got worse. I woke up four or five times a night in a cold sweat. I had no energy, and my body seemed to be always fighting off an infection.

I took trip after trip to my doctor, and we tested for everything. Nothing came back. He was completely stumped as to the cause of my problems.

We thought perhaps I had caught some tropical disease on my travels, so I went to an infectious disease specialist. No luck. We tried an ear, nose, and throat guy. Nothing. We tried other specialists and nothing there.

Along the way, I had an intuitive thought. "Doctor, please x-ray me because I think the hospital left the bullet inside me."

"Save your money," he replied. "They are crazy at the hospital you were in, but not that crazy."

Finally, I went to a gastroenterologist who wanted to do an entire upper and lower GI series. As I was getting ready, the nurse noticed my scar and inquired about the cause. I told her about the surgery for the gunshot wound, and she went ahead with my testing.

About twenty minutes later, she came back in, holding up my x-ray. "I see they left the bullet inside you," she mentioned casually. "Is that because it's located right next to your spine?"

Imagine my shock, then anger. I had been sick for months. I had no insurance, and had spent everything I had on doctors, tests, and specialists. I hadn't had a good night's sleep for so long I couldn't remember. And to think that the doctor had actually told me they took the bullet out! How could he lie to me like that?

I was confused and not sure where to turn. I had malpractice lawyers lined up to take my case. It looked like a sure out-of-court settlement for a million dollars easy.

But this was after I discovered *The Dynamic Laws of Prosperity* book. So I did what I always did when I needed guidance: I just closed my eyes, flipped the pages, and stuck my finger in to select a passage. It was on forgiveness.

And that section of the book actually discussed situations like being in a lawsuit with someone. The author wrote that you couldn't forgive someone if you were suing them, and that if you were holding onto resentment or revenge, you couldn't be open to receiving all your allotment of prosperity. I saw my million dollars disappearing.

Yet intuitively, I knew the author's words to be true. I spent about thirty minutes meditating on the situation. I realized that the doctors and medical team had taken out my appendix and left the bullet in for whatever reason. But they had also saved my life.

I had been shot in a robbery and taken to the hospital after losing a great deal of blood. My pulse was dropping, and my heart had almost stopped beating. If they didn't intervene, I would have died. I realized that they had done the best they could with what they had to work with.

I wrote out an affirmation of forgiveness thirteen times and put it in my Bible to pray on. I released the resentment, and viewed the doctors and medical people in the light of God. Then, an amazing thing happened.

That night, I got a complete night's sleep, without waking up in the middle of it for the first time since I could remember. I soon had another operation to have the bullet removed, but my health started improving dramatically on the day I forgave. Now I'm forty-eight, and I'm in the best health I've been in since I was twenty.

I came to understand that if you can't forgive someone, you can't be open for abundance. If you are holding on to revenge, love can't walk in. If you are hanging on to resentment, you are hanging on to being a victim. And if you are holding on to being a victim, there's no space in your mind to be a victor.

I'll tell you another interesting lesson I learned: The first person you have to forgive is yourself.

I don't know why so many people have such difficulty forgiving themselves, but they do. And I did, too. But I came to understand that no matter how bad I thought I was, I had a Creator who had already forgiven me. And I knew that I must forgive myself and move on, or I would continue to manifest a life of misery, limitation, and lack.

Once I did that, I started to manifest prosperity in the other areas of my life. I stopped repeating a lifelong pattern of negative, dysfunctional relationships. I attracted people who bring joy and meaning to my life. I've discovered my assignment, and do work I really love. And I've traded in being broke for being a multimillionaire.

But my prosperity work has taught me that there are actually seven prosperity laws you must live by. They are all interrelated. The Vacuum Law of Prosperity is in effect in forgiveness situations. When someone comes to me with his or her prosperity blocked, I recommend these three simple steps: 1) Mentally forgive everyone you are out of harmony with. 2) Mentally ask for forgiveness from the people you have wronged in the past, gossiped about, or are involved in lawsuits or other disharmony with. 3) If you have accused yourself of failure or mistakes, forgive yourself.

Once these three steps are completed, the rich avenue of divine prosperity will open wide for you!

Randy Gage

Life Lesson #1:
Don't Take It Personally

Do you sometimes feel like there is a conspiracy, and the whole world is picking on you? Your friends, family, colleagues, even strangers? You know they are really talking about you, even though they are making general statements. Who do they think they're kidding? Strangers even seem to be going out of their way to make your day difficult. You've been bumped with shopping carts and cut off on the road by inconsiderate people. Sound a little familiar? Here is the question—is everyone *really* out to get you, or is it your own baggage that makes you perceive that everyone has an agenda with your name on it?

Is it possible people are just carrying on with their lives, and the things that are happening are just . . . happening? Perhaps people really *are* speaking in generalities, but you are taking it personally.

Here's a scenario: Glen is driving home from work in his sleek, low-to-the-ground sports car. He's had an incredibly bad day and cannot wait to get home and relax. He is almost near his exit and needs to merge from the middle lane to get to the off ramp. He puts on his signal, sees an opening, and starts to go for it when the person behind him jumps right in. Glen is livid! He calls the person a few well-chosen names and stews about it the rest of the way home. Glen knows the person behind him did it on purpose.

In reality, the person behind Glen did not notice his signal. He was not sure how to reach his destination and asked his wife for directions. At the last minute, she realized that their exit was fast approaching and told him to get over right away. He was not out to "get" Glen. He never even saw Glen. Talk about two different perceptions of the same situation!

Earlier this week, a deer darted out from the woods as Glen was driving. The deer bounced off the top of the car, spun around, and returned to the woods from where it came. Just yesterday, as Glen was pulling into his driveway after a long day, he heard that all-too-familiar sound of pavement scraping the bottom of his beautiful car. Glen was not having a wonderful week. Funny, though, in these instances, Glen was not pleased at what occurred, but he did not blame the deer or the pavement, or swear that the deer was out to "get" him. If someone had suggested such an idea to Glen, he might have considered it silly. It never occurred to him to take these situations personally, yet he was completely convinced that the other driver in the first scenario was personally out to get him. Is the answer because it was a person and not a thing? Probably. If so, Glen should work on changing his perspective.

What might a change in perspective accomplish for Glen? For starters, he would not be in a bad mood about being cut off. It might also help him lighten up and relax. It takes a great deal of emotional energy to be angry and defensive. Glen would probably also laugh a little more. When you stop taking things personally, you can see the humor in situations. A change in perspective could make a dramatic difference in his life. What about yours?

So, what different perspective can you hold with people who mean no more harm to you than the deer or the pavement did to Glen? It can be different for each person. Will it be tolerance, acceptance, or perhaps even forgiveness?

Exercise

1. At the top of a clean page in your Prosperity Journal, write the name of a person that you've felt resentful toward lately.
2. Write down the perspective you currently hold about that situation.
3. Next, ask yourself, what's a different perspective I might hold about this situation that would feel better to me?
4. Try to identify at least six different perspectives.
5. Now, read through each perspective and ask yourself which perspective feels best?
6. When you've felt even a small sense of relief in how you feel, you've done your work!

The next time you find yourself reacting like Glen, try exploring a few different perspectives as an exercise to find the one that works best for you—the one that will help you shrug it off and *not* take it personally. You'll be amazed at how simply you can change the quality of your life just by changing perspectives!

Life Lesson #2
Where Thought Goes, Energy Flows

Have the daring to accept yourself as a
bundle of possibilities and undertake the
game of making the most of your best.

Henry Emerson Fosdick

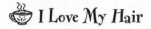 I Love My Hair

···

Remember, whatever game you play, 90 percent
of success is from the shoulders up.

MILFRED "DEACON" PALMER

I was born with a condition known as cleft palate. It's a malformation of the face, which involves the roof of the mouth, the upper lip, and the nose. Four surgeries by the time I was five, speech therapy through grade six, dental work, braces, consultations, more dental work, braces again, rhinoplasty, more dental work, temporary retainers, caps on my teeth, more caps on my teeth—you get the picture.

Hearing the news that there were further problems meant that I was going to spend countless hours in the dental office, as well as thousands of dollars I did not have. It was very emotional for me every time I would go through this process. It was as if all the strength I had mustered all those years of my childhood would leave me, and I would be reduced to the scared, vulnerable child I never allowed myself to be.

Through my younger years dealing with these issues, my parents taught me to be strong. They were coached by my doctors to make me strong. "Kids will make fun of Cathy. You must teach her to be strong," they'd tell my parents. "Be a little tougher with Cathy than your other children.

The world will be a little tougher on her, so make her strong," they suggested.

My parents did a very good job of it. I was outgoing, friendly, and fun. I had many friends; I was popular and well liked. I acted as if I were no different than any other child. I was *strong*.

Once when a classmate who did not know me well asked how my nose got that way, I made up a story about how I had been in a horrible car accident. At the time it sounded more glamorous than, "It's the way I was born!" You should have seen her face as I spun my fib.

I missed most of my art classes the entire time I was in elementary school because I had to attend speech lessons instead. This did not make me happy, as I missed the opportunity to design and create a special tile for the entryway of our elementary school. The tiles all the other kids in my class made are still embedded in the wall of the J. P. Oldham School. There's not a single one from me, though.

When a secret crush, and one of the cutest guys in the sixth grade, made fun of me in front of other kids, I laughed it off and then went home crying to my parents because my feelings were so hurt. I remember my dad telling me the boy was a very small person for treating me that way. I said, "But, Dad, he is the tallest kid in the class." I knew what he really meant, but it was easier to pretend. Still, I stayed strong.

Overall, I did well. I grew up, got my teeth fixed, had my nose fixed, stopped needing to go to speech class, and I was happy. I had a loving family and lots of friends, and I moved on with my life. I grew up, moved to California, went to college, graduated with a doctorate degree, married a wonderful man, opened a business, and was a very happy person. And I was still—strong.

Until the day I heard those dreaded words from my dentist, "Cathy, you have a problem." And I cried.

That was the first breakthrough for me. I knew something was changing; I had never cried at the dentist before.

I summoned my courage, committed to acting as if everything would be okay, and made an appointment to consult with the specialist. I knew that even though I was in for a journey I did not necessarily feel comfortable taking, I had to trust that this was in my best interest, and that I was going to be supported and guided through this.

Then, the magic began.

Within two to three weeks of receiving my unwelcome news, a woman I had known for quite some time became a new patient in my office. I am a chiropractic physician. I thought it curious that this particular woman was coming to see me, as I knew she had been seeing a respected colleague of mine for more than fifteen years. She told me she was looking for someone who could fulfill her needs in a different way. I commenced the consultation and, boy, was I in for a surprise!

As it so happened, this woman explained to me she was just about to embark on a long series of dental procedures. She was having extensive work done to correct some problems she had been emotionally unable to correct previously. As a young woman, she had experienced a trauma that involved her mouth, and when she would try to go for help, her emotional wound would open and she could never find the strength to complete the work. She now had found the strength and was prepared to begin the work. The most important part of her story was that she was excited about it! She told me she could not wait to get started!

I was, to say the least, astounded! I had only just begun to act as if all would be in my highest interest, and that I would be guided and supported through this experience. Here was proof of my affirmation sitting right in front of me, and it only took three weeks!

I had to know her secret.

As I had known her for some time and was very comfortable with her, I shared with her that I was having a similar experience in my life. Unlike her, I explained, I was not excited. In fact, the entire experience was emotionally charged, and not in a positive way!

"I have just the thing for you," she said.

Later that day, she dropped by the office with Lynn Grabhorn's book, *Excuse Me, Your Life Is Waiting*. She instructed me to read chapter twelve, "Thirty Days to

Breakthrough." I could not wait to get home and read!

Chapter twelve described a technique called Flip Switching. It is a release technique, one that allows for permanent release of emotional attachments to experiences, fears, phobias, and recurring issues. I skipped right over the lovely part where the author explained the theory and her experience with the techniques and went right to work.

"Make a list of thirty things you love about you," the instructions read. *I can do that,* I thought to myself.

"Each day for the next thirty days, choose one of the items on the list that you are attracted to. This will be your affirmation for the day." *Sounds easy.*

"Every time any type of emotion arises in your mind in regards to your issue, replace the thought with your affirmation of the day from the list of thirty things you love about yourself. At the end of thirty days, you will be emotionally released." *Really?*

Wow! Just thirty days, and I could release myself from thirty-plus years of emotional pain? Count me in!

I sat down and feverishly wrote for thirty minutes. I had my list, and in the number-one position I wrote, "I love my hair." It was a particularly good hair day that day! I probably should have written something deeper like, "I love my compassion for humanity," but I gotta tell you, "I love my hair" worked just fine.

The next morning, I began to follow Lynn's instructions

as soon as I awakened. My appointment for the consultation was about a week away. My impending dental work was constantly on my mind, along with its trusted companions: fear, anxiety, sadness, and sorrow. *I love my hair.* While brushing my teeth, my thoughts drifted, but once again I repeated, *I love my hair.* I drove to work. *I love my hair, I love my hair, I love my hair.* I had a full schedule of patients that morning. *Gee, Mary has nice teeth. I don't, but I love my hair.* I went to lunch, and had some free time to think, to feel the fear. I love my hair.

I must have recited that affirmation 5,000 times on Day One. It was exhausting, but *I loved my hair.*

On Day Two, I picked a new affirmation, but halfway through the day, I forgot what it was, so I fell back on Day One, as the author had suggested. *I love my hair.* I noticed that Day Two brought me less need for affirmation. *Could this really be working and so fast?*

Day Three, *Hey, this is getting easier.*

Day Four, *I love my hair so much!*

Day Five, *I have the best damn hair in the Universe!*

By Day Seven, I swear, I could not find one iota of fear, sadness, or pain anywhere around this issue. How was this possible? To me, it was a miracle! I was released! Who needed thirty days?

Finally, the day of my consultation arrived. I stepped up to the reception desk and received a warm welcome. I sat down to fill out my paperwork and was asked by a patient in the waiting room if I was there to see Dr. Paul. I said yes, I was. She proceeded to tell me what a wonderful dentist he is. She told me how happy I was going to be with his work, that he was a perfectionist but tons of fun, and I would be delighted with my experience. I was thrilled!

Next, I met his dental hygienist, who was to take preliminary x-rays. When she called my name, I looked in her direction, only to see a lovely blonde woman standing under a recessed light that shined down on her head and shoulders, making her look like an angel! I actually laughed out loud!

I am happy to report that my experience was more than delightful. Dr. Paul was wonderful. I was able to speak openly with him about my fears and the emotional pain I was feeling from all those years of being strong. He listened! He understood! He shared some of his own personal experiences with the dental work he had received. With his help and encouragement, and that of his wonderful staff and a wonderful releasing technique called Flip Switching, I was free at long last. You should see my smile!

And, oh yes, I really *do* love my hair!

Catherine Ripley Greene, D.C.

LIFE LESSON #2:
WHERE THOUGHT GOES, ENERGY FLOWS

Take a guess at the answer to the following question: How much time do you spend thinking about positive things versus negative things? Also consider the amount of time spent discussing days that are less than perfect, spouses who are less than perfect, and coworkers who are never perfect. Does it seem like 50/50, 20/80, or 80/20? The average person spends a substantial amount of time discussing and pondering the negatives that have occurred over the positives. Can you see the danger that results from participating in this pastime? Doubt, fears, negative beliefs, and undermining are a few to start with. If you've been a practitioner of negative focus, don't be alarmed. There is hope through reprogramming.

Negativity can seep into every aspect of life and take it over. Don't let it go on for another minute. Revamp the thinking process. Focus on the positive, change your scenery, change your friends, and be prepared to make whatever changes are necessary to move you a full 180 degrees.

By eliminating negative thoughts and negative focus from your life, it allows you to reclaim and remold your present. Imagine more stress-free time to spend with your family, the self-confidence to get out and meet new people, or the money that could come from a new promotion. One's attitude is one's calling card. It's so much easier to achieve success when you are approachable. So if you deem it necessary, why not make a clean sweep of your life and revamp your outlook? Test it out, even if on a trial basis.

Exercise

Give positive actions, positive thoughts, and positive companions your undivided attention for just a one-month period. As great things happen, mark them down in your Prosperity Journal, and review your list frequently. You'll soon become addicted to the success that begins flooding your way. By all means, open those positive floodgates!

Reprinted by permission of Off the Mark and Mark Parisi. ©2005 Mark Parisi.

Life Lesson #3
Seeing the Glass Half-Full

To be upset over what you don't have
is to waste what you do have.

Ken S. Keyes, Jr., Handbook to Higher Consciousness

☕ The Healing Power of Intention

Our intention creates our reality.

WAYNE DYER

Try as I might, my knee still wouldn't bend. It had been months since my accident in March. While walking across the street, I had been hit by a car.

I'd had surgery to reconnect the ligaments in my knee and spent eight weeks wearing a cast to mend my broken leg. Once the cast was removed and the surgery had healed, under my orthopedic doctor's guidance I would lay on my stomach night after night as my husband pushed on my leg to bend the knee, but to no avail. The leg was as stiff as a board. I was forced to walk with a cane.

In August, my doctor recommended a procedure where I would be put under anesthesia and he would force the knee to bend. "This is going to hurt a lot," he said. "You will need to be on crutches for a long time, and even with all that, the knee will never bend enough for you to go up the stairs without dragging the injured leg."

A friend suggested that I counter the doctor's prediction with a scenario more to my liking. As I lay on the gurney in the hall in front of the operating room, I followed my friend's advice. Over and over I described to my husband, Steve, that the doctor would come out of the operating room, shouting for joy, "I can't believe it! The leg went all the way back!" Then, I told my husband, I would wake up pain-free and say, "I don't need the crutches at all."

About ten minutes before I was wheeled into the operating room, I looked up at my husband and said, "You know what, Steve? I don't believe anything I'm saying."

"Oh," he responded, "then what do you believe?"

"I think it will be just as the doctor said. It will hurt a lot, and I will need to be on crutches for a long time. And even with all that, the knee will never bend enough for me to go up the stairs without dragging my leg," I said.

"Okay," Steve said, serenely. "Now go back to the other story."

At that moment, something strange happened to my consciousness. I expected Steve to agree with the realistic expectation set by the doctor. When he didn't, my mind went into total confusion, then emptiness, and then to a simple openness. I returned to the positive story.

After the procedure, the doctor came out of the operating room and said to Steve, "I can't believe it! The leg went all the way back!"

I woke up feeling pain-free and wonderful and, while we took the crutches to please the hospital staff, I didn't need them. Today, I am a yoga teacher. I use this experience as an anchor to remind me of the potential power of affirmation, visualization, and clear intention to affect reality.

Kathleen Carroll

LIFE LESSON #3:
SEEING THE GLASS HALF-FULL

When a whole lot of things are not going your way, it can be quite difficult to find a bit of optimism—seemingly impossible, in fact. But hold on, do you remember the old adage, "Is the glass half-empty or half-full?" Well, it serves a dual purpose. If you find yourself thinking that the glass really is half-empty, it serves as a wake-up call to the need for an attitude adjustment. On the other hand, if you think the glass is half-full, then you've just touched on another of the natural laws—the Law of Polarity.

The Universal Law of Polarity is like a self-inflicted reality check. It's a glimpse into the other side, typically the bright, fun, successful side that is the equal and exact opposite to the dark, boring, and failure-ridden side. It helps minimize negative vibrations that, when left to reverberate on their own, make it harder to move away from. Instead, when polarity is applied, positive vibrations are created, making it all but impossible to stay pessimistic. Almost an instant dose of sunshine!

Life Lesson #4
Letting Go to Let It Flow

Money is neither my god nor my devil.
It is a form of energy that tends
to make us more of who we already are,
whether it's greedy or loving.

Dan Millman

There Is Enough Money for Everyone

A billion here and a billion there,
and pretty soon you're talking real money.

EVERETT DIRKSEN

My husband and I were in a complete state of financial lack—both in our beliefs and in our bank account. We had over $35,000 in credit-card debt, and both of us were unemployed. At the same time, we were beginning to study and understand the Law of Attraction and how we were creating a lot more of what we did not want: debt!

Although we were not learning these principles and laws in direct relationship to finances, we started to apply them to our experience with money. The following is much of what we learned, summarized.

Money is a system of energy. It is a neutral energy with a belief and perception we have each placed on it. Air is also energy, yet most people do not believe in a lack of air. When you breathe in air, do you panic because you fear that there may not be enough so you better count your breaths to make sure you don't run out? Do you scold your children for taking in too many breaths and using too much air? Do you worry that you might run out of air at the end of the day, or week, or month? Probably not, but if you did you would suffer from breathing difficulties and have to closely manage your air intake.

Most of the money we exchange every day is no longer currency but numbers on a piece of paper. The amount of money you have or don't have is directly related to your beliefs about money. A lot of people believe there is not enough money, and their life reflects that belief. Every time you spend money, what feelings do you have? Do you feel good or worried? Do you worry you shouldn't be spending the money because you are thinking about how much you do not have, or are you thinking: "I love to spend money because there is enough money for everyone, and I always flow a lot into my life"?

Because of our agency, we are free to create any belief we want. Tell yourself: "I am wealthy, and I am spiritual. I am allowing money to flow easily into my life, and I am using it to enrich my life and the lives of others. I am wealthy, and I am obedient to God's will for me. I am a humble, prosperous servant of the Lord. I am grateful for all the abundance that flows to me on all levels. I am healthy and experiencing a life of grace and ease, and I am spiritual." What would happen if these were your beliefs?

Every time we have an interaction with money, the Universe is giving us a chance to clear the deeper beliefs of not enough and the feeling of fear from our cells. Some people believe money comes easily, and they will always have enough. Many people believe in a lack of money and continue to create an abundance of lack.

My husband and I began to identify our beliefs about money and realized that we were creating our own lack with money and poverty consciousness. These beliefs included:

- I will never make enough money.
- I am always in debt.
- My parents never had enough, and I never will either.
- Money always goes out faster than it comes in.
- I am always worrying about money because there is never enough.

We also realized that many of our beliefs about money were woven into our spiritual beliefs. Some of our most common beliefs included:

- Money is filthy, dirty, and evil.
- I am poor, but righteous.
- There are too many poor people for me to deserve wealth.
- Only people who cheat have money.
- I have a fear of being greedy.
- Poverty keeps me humble.

If you are experiencing a lack of money, and the experience of managing money is a constant struggle that you regularly wrestle with in your mind, you have deeper beliefs and patterns with money that are keeping you stuck in a state of lacking. Poverty consciousness can be easily changed to prosperity consciousness by clearing your deeper beliefs and replacing them with new ones. Some of the new beliefs we began to embrace and practice included:

- I recognize prosperity everywhere and rejoice in it fully. There is plenty for me.
- The abundance of the Universe is available to everyone, including me.
- I spend money wisely and comfortably.
- I am open and receptive to new avenues of income.
- I am comfortable with large sums of money.
- I am using money to bless my life and others.
- I am wealthy, generous, and spiritual.
- I am a money magnet; I am attracting my piece of the prosperity that God has provided for everyone.
- I am worthy and deserving of large sums of money.
- I continuously rejoice in and bless the good fortune of everyone.

As well as establishing new beliefs, you will create new behaviors with money. If someone were to ask you, "Do you have any money?" what would be your most common response? If it is frequently "No," then you are telling the Universe you have no money, and you will continue to have no money. Always carry money in your wallet or billfold. Always be able to answer, "Yes, I have money. I have plenty of money." That is the message that will help you create more money. Whenever you spend money, notice how you feel. If you feel uncomfortable and nervous because you are worried that the money you are spending might not be replaced, the signal you are sending out is one of lack, and lack will be returned to you.

When you spend money, create a positive, peaceful feeling and trust that as you spend money, you create a vacuum for more money to come into your life. Always stay within your current means of income, and at the same time create a vibration of prosperity to create more coming in the future. Every time you pay your bills, be in the energy of gratitude that you have creditors that trust you and offer you their services. Acquire sound money-management skills to assist you in staying in integrity with your money.

When you communicate about money, do you talk about not having enough and focus your words on lack and struggle with money? Notice your communication patterns with money and choose to speak positively about your state of abundance with money. Do you trust your family members and perceive them as capable and competent when it comes to spending money? Or do you fear that they will create debt and spend more than you have so you need to control them? Create perceptions and language that reflect a state of prosperity consciousness rather than poverty consciousness.

The Universe does not know your bank account status; it only reads the signals you are feeding it. So create a vibration of wealth by playing the following game:

Pretend you have an unlimited supply of $100 bills in your wallet. Every time you spend a $100 bill, imagine another one magically replacing it. Throughout your day, think of the many things you could spend that $100 on. Act as if you are spending it over and over and over. Rejoice and have fun with all the things you could buy, all the people you could share it with, and all the experiences you could create.

As you do this, you will send out a vibration of wealth and prosperity that will assist you in creating more wealth.

As you shift into a vibration of prosperity consciousness, you will create and attract new avenues and opportunities for more money to come into your life. Money is a resource that God has given us to bless our lives, not to interfere with our daily happiness. If you are creating your experience with money as a negative distraction, choose to clean it up. Create money to be like your experience with air, something you know there is plenty of for you and everyone else. Money, like air, is a resource to assist you in creating and sustaining a life of joy and happiness. You never worry about air; you just trust and let it be there for you. Stop worrying about money and start trusting that you will be provided for. Trust that you will make choices to manage it in a way that blesses your life.

As a result of the changes we made in our beliefs and through practicing these new tools, my husband attracted a new job that paid him six figures, we were able to pay off our debt within a year, and we are now more prosperous and wealthy than we have ever been, for which I am deeply grateful!

Carol Tuttle

LIFE LESSON #4: LETTING GO TO LET IT FLOW

Magnetism is a wonderful thing. We often hear that someone has a *magnetic personality*, or that they are full of magnetism, even that opposites attract like magnets. Why this fascination with magnetism? Perhaps because the term *magnetism* implies that the opportunity exists for something to be drawn to you easily and effortlessly. What if that thing is success, fame, or money?

The majority of the population craves money, but most people feel they don't have enough of it. Why is that? Since we know how strong the powers of attraction are, and that like attracts like, the answer lies in the perception that "most people feel they don't have enough of it."

For example, let's suppose you are facing a bag of

money. You *really* want that bag of money. You stand there thinking of all the things you can't afford because you don't have the bag of money. You focus on all the things you can't be, do, or have. You feel frustrated, and you turn away from the bag of money.

Then you begin to think about how you would like to have it. You think of all the positive things you would like to do with it, and you start vibrating positive thoughts. At this point, the Law of Attraction says that you are *now* in a place where you can attract the bag of money. You have become a money magnet.

When you take a snapshot of your current scenario, can you state with sincerity that you are magnetizing money? Have you let go of any limiting beliefs that you have about money? Do you believe financial success is something that happens to others, or that you are undeserving? If money and financial success are your goals, how can you become that all-powerful magnet?

Let go and simply allow it!

Allow yourself to *let go* of any negative thoughts and limiting beliefs that have blocked your success. Allow yourself to believe that you can have the success you desire. Allow yourself to have the courage to pursue the avenues that will lead you to your financial success. Allow yourself to magnetize the people and scenarios that will help your team assemble effortlessly. Allow your spirit to dance with the knowledge that you have the power to bring what you want to fruition.

You do have what it takes to become a money magnet. You just have to believe in yourself, believe in your goals, and trust that the Universe will do its part once you've done yours.

Exercise:

1. Draw a line down the middle of a clean page in your Prosperity Journal.
2. At the top of the page, write: My Current Limiting Thoughts About Money.
3. In the left-hand column of the page make a list of all your current limiting thoughts you have about money.
4. On the right-hand column of the page, reach for a better-feeling thought about money.

Life Lesson #5
Empower Yourself for Success

What you become is far more important
than what you get. What you get will be
influenced by what you become.

Jim Rohn

☕ Until You Value Yourself . . .
Don't Expect Anyone Else To

Don't compromise yourself.
You are all you've got.

BETTY FORD

Ever since I was seventeen years old and almost died of strychnine poisoning, I had dreamed of being an inspired teacher, healer, and philosopher. The dream came when I had the opportunity to meet an amazing teacher who inspired me to tears, as he had millions of others around the world.

I decided then that I wanted to step foot on every country on the face of the Earth and share my research findings with millions of people to help them live amazing, abundant lives. Today, after thirty-four years of persistent effort, I am certainly living my teenage dream. My life is blessed, and I have been greatly rewarded. But along the journey there were many lessons to be learned and many challenges to be faced.

One such lesson that impacted me deeply and permanently was the time I finally began charging fees for my various teaching services. I had to overcome the fear of being rejected for requesting and receiving money, and for amply valuing my fledgling educational services. I was unquestionably minimizing my financial destiny.

There I was, twenty-three years of age, already teaching and tutoring other students "freely" out of my apartment, but one night something began shifting my financial perspective. A great lesson concerning money, fair exchange, and self-value was about to be revealed.

In my one-bedroom apartment in Pasadena, Texas, twenty-one students crowded together in my living and dining rooms, eager to listen to my inspired ideas concerning mind/body interactions, specifically those involving inner healing. That night, because my college tuition and living expenses were mounting and I had a growing desire to build a vast library of books, I experienced a psychological and soon-to-come financial shift.

I decided to place a bowl on my dining-room table with a small sign on it stating: "Love Donation." At the end of my three-hour presentation, I watched everyone begin to leave. Only five dollars had been placed in the Love Donation bowl. I looked at the bowl with some despair since I was hoping to receive much more, but the bowl had been ignored or overlooked by most attendees when they were departing. That night I thought that I was not going to be able to afford to buy more books, pay my rent, or continue classes unless something shifted.

At first, I became mad at the attendees, and then I

realized it was all about my fear of asking for what I wanted and feeling unworthy of receiving it. At the next class, I decided to aim for a love donation of ten dollars. At the end of the night, ten dollars remained in the bowl. I decided to raise the amount to twenty dollars for the next class. By the end of that class, twenty-five dollars was left in the bowl.

I finally become more bold and decided that I was going to charge a minimum entrance fee of twenty dollars for each of my evening classes and do away with the love donation idea altogether.

On that night, once I firmly declared to myself and my attendees that I was charging a minimum fee, I was amazed to discover that 85 percent of the attendees gratefully placed their twenty dollars in the bowl. I looked at the bowl at the end of the evening with amazement and tears of gratitude, for I somehow knew that I had discovered a great lesson along the road to my dreams.

What an amazing lesson! It was as if the world was trying to tell me to value my teaching services, and myself, but until that night I had been unwilling to listen. The moment that I did is the same moment that I received. From that night onward, I have remembered this great financial lesson, and I have raised my fee every year since. Today, I receive a lovely honorarium for my teaching services, which have spread throughout the world.

No one valued my services until I valued myself. Wow,

what a great and yet simple financial lesson to finally learn!

Until you value yourself, don't expect anyone else to. Until you pay yourself first, don't expect anyone else to. Until you allow yourself to do what you dream of, don't expect anyone else to encourage you to.

Once you declare your fee—with a no-turning-back certainty—the world will respond with a level of prosperity and abundance like never before. Today, I do what I love and love what I do. I get handsomely paid to teach and travel across the world, and I am abundantly prosperous in many more ways than one.

Dr. John F. Demartini

LIFE LESSON #5: EMPOWER YOURSELF FOR SUCCESS

Do you know that you have the power to succeed at everything you do right now, this minute? Are you surprised? Your thoughts control the actions that create your successes or failures. So if your thoughts are the foundation for success, if you spend some time focusing on the type of thoughts that are typically manifested and the ones that create success, you'll have the tools necessary for self-empowerment.

When it's time to try something new, do you run right out and jump into it, confident that you are going to succeed with no doubts? Isn't that a wonderful picture? But, unfortunately, much of the population first has to contend with a little negative self-talk, a personal gremlin. Are you familiar with the gremlin? Perhaps you know him or her by a different name. The gremlin waits to shoot down our ideas, deflate our elation, and sabotage our plans . . . when we allow it to happen.

Often, this negativity is so commonplace that we don't even recognize it when it is occurring; therefore, we are unable to stop it. So, when we carry on with our activities, we are often full of doubt, harboring feelings of incompetence, and brandishing insecurities that are in essence setting us up for failure—or at the very least a much more difficult road toward success. The worst-case scenario is when we allow our gremlins to stop us from even trying to reach our goal. So how do we silence the gremlin and replace it with our own personal cheerleader instead? There are several ways.

Exercise

Learn to recognize the gremlin for what it is: a thief that stifles creativity, hinders success, and paralyzes growth. Begin to listen carefully for that voice and cut it off before its effects can take root. Here are some ideas:

1. Wear a rubber band on your wrist for a month and giving yourself a "zing" whenever you hear that gremlin beginning to discourage you. Talk about a reminder! We'd rather zing the gremlin than ourselves any day!

2. Surround yourself with positive, happy people who do not allow gremlins to steal their successes. First, it becomes very difficult to continuously hear about positive things without some of your own to add. You'll start looking for ways to join the crowd. Second, the more you are around positive thoughts, the more real they become, and the more you attract the same back to you.

3. Recall the times when you successfully combated your gremlin and let those instances serve as your road map. Write about these times in your Prosperity Journal. Writing things down allows you

to explore the feelings, thoughts, and circumstances that surrounded the experience. Details that are typically glossed over when focusing on part of the big picture can be extremely beneficial when later explored. Knowing that you have what it takes to face any challenges and overcome your obstacles is just the thing to bolster your confidence and self-esteem—two of the things that gremlins seem to sap out of their victims. Don't be a victim any longer; be a victor.

So are you ready to step up to the challenge? We know you can do it! Learning how to silence your gremlin is a tool that will be beneficial for life. Isn't it time to empower yourself and position yourself to succeed at all you set out to accomplish? Yes, yes, and yes!

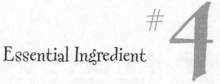

INSPIRED ACTIONS

To will is to select a goal, determine a course
of action that will bring one to that goal, and
then hold to that action till the goal is
reached. The key is action.

Michael Hanson

Life Lesson #1
First Things First

Thought is the blossom; language the bud;
action the fruit behind it.

Ralph Waldo Emerson

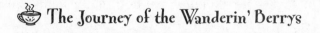

The Journey of the Wanderin' Berrys

Trust—expecting the best to happen,
believing in your ability to create what you want,
and knowing you deserve to have it—can be
demonstrated in many ways. It is demonstrated
by believing in something even when the outer
world seems to reflect something else.

SANAYA ROMAN AND DUANE PACKER

On December 23, 2007, my family celebrated our four-year "New Life" anniversary. It has been three years since we left all we knew in our outer life and began an internal and external journey to reclaim what we had forgotten in our inner life. Reflecting on these last three years and where we have come as a family, I see that my fears were unfounded. I worried that when we stopped traveling and settled down somewhere, we'd forget what we learned on our magical odyssey. However, what we did is staying with us, and I sense it will stay with us forever.

We had a beautiful home in a desirable mountain town dubbed the "Paris of the South." We lived in a 1916 farmhouse on two acres with historic oaks and heirloom rose gardens. My husband, Peter, had just received a promotion in his work for Toshiba, and I had a successful energy-work practice. The kids were attending the best public school in Asheville, where Peter and I were active volunteers. We grew organic fruits and vegetables on our land, and had a delightful community of friends. From the outside, our life looked really good, and in many ways it was.

But, on the inside, there were subtle messages that something was out of balance. Pete was caught up in the status of his job, chasing down a dream of success that never quite seemed to materialize. We loved our home and land, but it took so much work to maintain it. We spent every available dollar on repairs and renovations. We spent every available moment working on the gardens, the house, or the yard. When we weren't working, we felt guilty that we should be. We were losing touch with each other and growing apart. We had dreamed of having family time together, but what we created was something always needing to be done. We did not hang out together unless we were all working! Our children expressed their disappointment in different ways, but Pete and I were too caught up in the maintenance of the "dream."

Around September 2003, I began getting more urgent signals that a change was coming. I had been getting these messages of imbalance for years, but did not want to listen to them. As I felt the imbalance more acutely, I started to listen. The message was simple: *Let go.* But let go of what?

In October 2003, I attended a workshop, where the

question was asked, "If you are standing at a crossroads, what is written on the two signs?" This question was such a gift to me because I saw it so clearly. I was standing at a point in my life where I felt I had to choose between my deep, true life and spiritual path or Peter.

After some serious soul-searching and late-night/early-morning conversations with Peter, we decided that there was indeed something that needed to change. I shared my concerns and the vision I'd seen, and he was blown away. We realized that we needed to re-examine our priorities and look at where we had gotten off track. Our utter devotion early in our twenty-year relationship was to each other and to our family; we had such a profound awareness that love was all that mattered, and that the details of life were the gravy. What happened to our lives that we had forgotten this simple truth? It was here that we realized what we needed to do. We needed to radically change our lives and make up for some lost family/love time!

Over a few weeks of intense surrender, we saw where we needed to release our attachments and our fears. My office downtown was the first casualty. Oh, so painful to let that go! But the bliss and clarity that followed was the reward. Soon after, Peter got the message to let go of his current job. His ego put up a fight for all of five minutes, when deeper sense took over. We kept breathing and releasing, as we were exquisitely guided as to what old aspect of our lives to let go of. Then, we realized it wasn't just about changing our work. In the still of one very powerful morning, we were told to let go of our home.

Our house never went on the market; the first person we told bought it. We then felt led to let go of our possessions. We were given a vision of the four of us as a family, standing naked on the edge of a cliff, hand in hand. We were giving ourselves the opportunity to remove all distractions and trappings in order to see clearly what was most important. We sold our possessions, opening our home for four weekends straight to friends and strangers who had heard about our story. The more we released, the clearer it became that we were to buy a motor home and travel the country together. The vision of where we were being led started to take some shape. The sense I got was that we were going to learn how to be a family in a different way than we had before. By late December, just weeks after we made the decision to change our lives, we drove out of Asheville in our recently purchased RV to begin our new life. Talk about fast manifestation!

We began having what we called "Pyramid Meetings," where we followed an internally guided structure of meditating, check-in, and family discussion (the Round Table). We asked questions of our inner guidance and discussed what we had each received. Our relationship shifted into one of four equal decision-makers, each with input that was valued and heeded. We traveled across the southern United States, being guided in our family meditations where next to point the immense nose of our RV. Do we go north today? West? Sometimes we would intuitively wind up in a place for one or two nights; other times we were guided to stay there for several months at a time. Sometimes we fell into volunteer positions as campground hosts or interpretive staff in national and state parks, where we got the opportunity to learn even more.

We learned that our home is in our hearts, and that our grounding came not from being rooted in any one physical location, but from our connection as a family and in ourselves. We re-learned how to be together, but in a stronger way, reclaiming the love for each other that we had begun to forget. We refused several invitations from well-meaning folks who thought that since we were living in a motor home we would travel to see them, but we really needed to honor the process of recovery we were experiencing as a family. In all situations, we were guided as a family to look for the gifts in every interaction. We learned that we truly make our life by our choice to be grateful for wherever we are and that we can learn something from every person we meet. We learned it is all about choice.

Eventually, we wound up in the San Luis Valley of Colorado. We feel that this valley is a very good energetic match for each of us. We feel that our physical journey prepared us for our life here, but the most significant travel happened in our hearts. We healed ourselves and mended the places in our family where the veneer of love was wearing thin. We learned to communicate in a different way, honoring each other as equal, infinite beings, each with gifts to bring to the world. All of us have found deep satisfaction in creating our lives from the inside out, rather than looking for cues from the outer world about what we are supposed to do with our time here on Earth. This has been a major awakening and blessing for us. But, best of all, we learned that there is nothing more important than love.

Licia Berry

LIFE LESSON #1:
FIRST THINGS FIRST

Inspiration hits both in good and bad times. When it's good, you may have an abundance of ideas. It can be overwhelming when the flood of ideas comes. When you're in the middle of contrast, there will be plenty of paths to take, but you may not be able to decide which one to choose. Until you have full access to your inner guidance, the choices can be both irresistible and overpowering.

What do you do? Choose one inspired action. No matter which action you take first, it must feel good. It may feel best to take the action that will give you the most relief. This choice will give you some immediate relief and breathing room. Your stress level will come down, and you will have greater access to your intuition.

If you feel a tinge of fear about all the action that you *perceive* will need to happen to manifest the desire, start small. If that credit-card debt is accumulating and you can't see your way out, take a step back. Breathe. If you were to take a tiny step forward, what would feel best? If the answer is to pay ten dollars over the minimum payment required, do it. You have to start somewhere. This simple action will be empowering.

Taking an inspired action toward a goal may generate the excitement that you may think you've lost.

Action can be very empowering, even when it's not directly related to a specific goal. This is called "coming in through the back door." It's a roundabout approach to boosting your belief level in your ability to attract exactly what you want. And it can happen while you're doing the simplest things.

You may feel inspired to take a walk to calm yourself. During the walk, you may have a great idea about your business. Inspired ideas and actions generate more inspired ideas and actions. That is how the Law of Attraction works.

Life Lesson #2
The Time Is Now

. . . .

It is the nature of thought
to find its way into action.

Christian Nevell Bovee

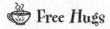 **Free Hugs**

> *The more you can dream, the more you can do.*
>
> MICHEAL KORDA

A few months back, Lisa Murray heard about a Free Hugs movement and decided to check it out on YouTube. As she watched Juan Mann's video of people just hugging him, she felt a sense of peace and inner calm come over her. She admits that, at first, she thought the video would be corny and the hugs forced, but after only a few moments she took off her skeptical sunglasses and watched in complete awe.

It was then that she decided to find out if she could do a Free Hugs campaign in her area. And that's just what she did! Once she found out one had not been done in the Hollywood, California, area, she was set on getting one done—immediately. Although her timing seemed a bit off (she had just had the first of two surgeries to battle cervical cancer just two days before the video was shot), she was determined to be the change the world needed!

So, as the people of Hollywood went about a normal day, they had no idea what was heading their way! For the next two hours of what would have been a normal day, these people were treated to Free Hugs. Two volunteers held up signs that said just that—Free Hugs—and they offered strangers a chance to receive their wonderful, heartfelt gift. As they did this, Lisa and her crew filmed a video that would receive national attention on such Internet sites as Yahoo and MySpace. It had over 30,000 hits the first night! Murray's "Free Hugs in Hollywood" video, which has generated over a million views, won a Yahoo! Veddy Award for "Best Documentary."

So what's the point in all this? Well, for two hours, people in and near this project witnessed something amazing. They saw people of all shapes, sizes, backgrounds, and race let down their guards and trust their fellow man and woman. And soon after, people all over the world got to see the positive effect of this simple, but not so simple gesture.

So, at a time that may not have been the best for Lisa, due to her battle with cancer (which she won), Lisa also benefited. In an amazing and overwhelming turn of events, the video produced a tremendous outpouring of e-mails and calls thanking her for acting on her inner voice and just doing it! Although Lisa was not a "hugger," she welcomed these Internet hugs and well wishes at a time when she most needed them. Who says timing isn't everything? It is always amazing what can happen when we follow that little voice that leads us into the unknown.

Lisa set out on this project to see what would happen, and happen things did! She has not only touched the lives of thousands and been flooded with e-mail, but she has also received interview requests for her upcoming documentary, "I Have Dreams, Dammit."

Lisa Murray set out to make the world a better place by offering a free hug, and what a difference those hugs have made! Cost of two poster boards . . . $3.00. Cost of two videotapes . . . $10.00. Chance to make the world a kinder, more peaceful place one hug at a time . . . Priceless.

Christine Brooks

LIFE LESSON #2: THE TIME IS NOW

When inspiration hits, a whirlwind of energy is yours, and sometimes the urge to be in action is great. If you've been wanting to take action in an area of your life for a while now, watch for clues. This type of inspiration hits with projects like cleaning out a closet or file cabinets, throwing a dinner party, planting bulbs for the spring, or shopping for paint to redo your bedroom.

When you're in the mood to take action, it feels so good. If you push yourself to do the same action when you're not inspired, get ready for a miserable time. You make mistakes, things take longer than they are supposed to, machinery and computers have snafus—anything that can get in the way, will.

Try sitting down at the computer to write when you're not feeling the vibe. Can you say, "Writer's block?" When you are forcing yourself to take action before you are ready, it is difficult to tap into intuition or creativity. That is why it is important to wait until the inspiration hits.

Timing and inspiration go together like peanut butter and jelly. It's a natural fit. It may feel unnatural for you to trust this timing if you are accustomed to making yourself do things whether you would like to or not. Let's say you have set your intentions for the day and written them down.

••

My intentions for today:

1. Call hotel for reservation
2. Write newsletter
3. Walk for 30 minutes
4. Start proposal for potential client
5. Help kids with school project
6. Attract solution for more income

••

When you look at your list, it feels as though there is not a lot of time to spare if you want to accomplish these outcomes. You get up and begin your morning practice. You're feeling pretty good, but you are focused on what you want to check off on your list first. You find yourself in the garage beginning to rearrange bicycles, car accessories, or gather clothes and random toys you plan on giving to charity. Then, you pick up a broom and begin sweeping.

You hear a gruff voice in your head say, "Get back to the list. You don't have time for this. You are getting side-tracked." Before the gremlin reared its ugly head, you were getting into this inspired cleaning. You hadn't planned on tidying up in the garage, but that's exactly where you found yourself, and it was feeling really good. Should you finish the job or get back to your list?

If you liked cleaning, continue cleaning. You were in the flow. Stay there. This is how it's supposed to feel. If you were trusting that whatever needed to get done today would get done, would you feel guilty for taking a detour in the garage? When you allow yourself the freedom of following inspiration, you will reap abundance in all things.

Inspiration can hit when it seems you are tapped out on time, money, and resources. If you're feeling a lack of any of these, then you will only get more of not enough time, money, and resources. Inspired actions create alignment within you when you honor them. When you are feeling good, no matter the thought or task at hand, you are magnetic to everything you want. Trust the timing.

Cynthia Loy Darst is a great example of following her inspiration while her life seemed very full. In 1997, she decided she would be in charge of putting together the world's largest coaching conference. She had no experience with such an event, except for being an attendee.

At the time of planning the conference, she was running her own business, appropriately called The Inspiration Point. She was also a lead trainer at the Coaches Training Institute, serving on the board of the International Coach Federation, was married, *and* in the process of moving. That's a very full plate!

When asked what came over her to take on such a large year-long project while she had so many other things going on in her life, she replied: "I had a very strong vision about bringing the coaching community together. I decided that by taking on the conference chair position, I would actually create *more* balance in my life. If I couldn't figure out what to do next, I would bring myself back to the vision. The next step would always be revealed to me when I would state the vision. I had a lot of support to tap into, and I would call them when I got stuck."

There is no such thing as bad timing when it comes to inspired actions. When you utilize your "trust muscle" and follow the impulses and ideas, you will learn to drop everything. You will be served well. If some part of the idea feels funky, or not in alignment with your personal values, most likely it is not an inspired action. You can always tweak the idea or action to be in alignment. *All* the pieces must feel good or it's a "no go."

Inspired action must feel good *during* and *after* it is taken. Keep in mind that it's okay to feel a bit anxious *before* you embark on some actions; a bit of trepidation is natural at the beginning. If you were inspired to skydive, you'll likely feel butterflies when you step into the plane that you are about to jump out of! Once out of the plane, however, you may well have a smile on your face during the whole freefall. After you land safely on the ground, you may be high-fiving everyone around you—not to mention the buzz you'll feel the rest of the day.

The other part of trusting timing is when the inspiration is not there. Inspiration can't be forced. It comes when it comes. If something doesn't happen when you think it should, relax. Sometimes you won't know until after the fact that the timing was indeed perfect.

What inspirations have you been putting off?

If you dropped the story about not having enough time, knowledge, money, or resources, would you go for your dream?

What would the inspired action give you?

Exercise:

Imagine you have completed all the tasks in your life that have a deadline attached to them. Your tax preparation has been completed. Projects for the kids, work, and house all have a checkmark next to them. Done! You've already got your body and finances in shape.

What would you spend your time doing? What would feel like a luxury? What have you been saying that you'll do someday when you have time? You may find you have many inspired ideas and desires. Make a list in your Prosperity Journal. Which one is calling you forth?

What if you took one action this week regarding this inspiration? What if you gave it fifteen minutes of your time? Do it. Just for the sheer joy of taking inspired action. See how it feels. Remember, maybe the inspired action is to read a fiction novel. Inspired action is not to be equated to productivity. It's supposed to feel good simply because you enjoy the action. Yes, the outcome might give you a feeling of accomplishment. But the purpose is truly joy.

Life Lesson #3
Stop, Look, and Listen

∙∙

Things do not happen;
things are made to happen.

John F. Kennedy

☕ Prosperity Starts at the Kitchen Table

In the middle of difficulty lies opportunity.

ALBERT EINSTEIN

It seemed that my life was over at the age of fifty-two. My marriage had failed, my business partner left, and my daughter's family moved away along with my adored grandsons. I felt empty and useless. The very people I loved the most and had served as frequent guests at my kitchen table had gone away from me. I sat alone at my empty kitchen table and stared out the window, attempting to understand and make some sense of the loss I felt.

Until then, there had been some very full, good years. As a Law of Attraction teacher, my focus had been about sharing how to use Strategic Attraction to attract more perfect relationships, and my life was filled with the people I loved. The kitchen table was always in use with my friends, family, and business associates who came to partake of the love being served. Now, with all of my significant relationships leaving, I was devastated.

A little pinhole of light shined into my darkness after many months of drifting with little energy to give to my life or business. I read an e-mail from a woman who wanted to know if I had a training program that would certify her to teach our Strategic Attraction methodology. I smiled. *If only she knew how I was really feeling.* The following day, another e-mail arrived with a second inquiry from a woman making a similar request. My mood picked up a bit, as I considered that there were actually two women requesting to be trained, yet I had no such program to offer.

The turning point came when a third person called the office to find out how she could be trained in our process, which she said had made a big difference in her life. Her enthusiasm was contagious! Even I was excited after speaking with her.

Now, my attention was drawn to these distinct signs— three women, all living in Houston, Texas, all requesting to be certified and trained within two weeks of each other. The message was undeniable! This was a blatant message to me that it was time to move my life in a new direction.

I met with each of the three women individually to hear about their inspiration and desires about how they wanted to use the training. It was inspiring to me that someone else saw this training as a possibility for themselves, especially at a time when I was feeling like nothing I believed in had any value. I promised each one that I would train them if they would be willing to participate in a pilot program that I would design as we went along.

Each agreed enthusiastically, and we met around my kitchen table every week for three months. For the first time that year, the kitchen table was alive with vibrant and enthusiastic people engaging in conversations. My heart was opening again as I basked in the love I felt for each person.

At our first meeting, each of us planted a cutting taken from a jade plant that I had as a symbol of new growth being started from the mother plant. From that moment on, I began to see a new meaning for my life. At the same time, each of the women began transforming their lives. It was a wonderful journey that gave me a new focus, and I began to look forward to every gathering. Gradually, my empty nest filled with new energy and purpose.

I still grieved for the loss of the significant relationships, yet I was able to forgive and let go of the past. I saw that this ending was part of a natural evolution necessary for me as much as for the well-being of each of the people who went their separate ways. It fell into perfect perspective with what I taught in Strategic Attraction, and in the very near future I would see how this was the impetus of building great internal strength for me.

The pilot program lit the fire that began to attract more people, and before the alpha program had completed, our beta program was launched as the first official program available to the public.

My newfound bliss opened the door for more beginnings and new relationships, which have been blessed with increased financial prosperity and abundance. Our business profits tripled the first year. This year we are expanding to include trainers in specific geographic areas, and increasing our academy of programs to include a wide variety of training materials. We still use the kitchen table for our most important planning sessions. It seems to be the perfect place where friends come together for the sustenance of what is most important—love.

Jan Stringer

Life Lesson #3:
Stop, Look, and Listen

Evidence is everywhere. You get to choose the evidence you want to collect. Would you like to support the belief that you are the queen or king of your life, or are you collecting proof that you'll never get what you want? It is guaranteed that you will always find a dozen or more reasons to support your focus of the moment.

Here is an example of how fast you can make up a story about something. You and your mate are having a wonderful afternoon. You're driving through the wine country, taking in the scenery. The conversation is rich and relaxed.

Then your mate, who is driving the car, slams on the brakes. *Argh! This always happens. She never pays attention. She knows I hate it when she gets too close to the car in front of us. How insensitive of her. She is always in her own world.*

The next thing you know, you bring up all the old data in your head about what a terrible driver your mate is. Next, you venture off into other thoughts about how she is less than perfect. Before you know it, you've started questioning your sanity for being with this person. This all unfolds in four minutes flat. Whew! That was intense!

So goes the human mind. It's an expert at collecting data. But is it the data you want? Does it bring you in alignment with what you want, or have you been collecting proof that it's hard to attract your desire? Stop. Breathe. Ah, yes. Take a deep breath in and out. Again. How are you feeling? If you look out into your world, what clues are being shown to you about your next inspiration?

If you are willing to look for the evidence that there is an obvious next step, you will see it. Sometimes, you have to listen for it. Your inner guidance has been telling you, but you can't hear over the gremlin's dooming voice. The truth is that at any given moment, you have access to the next inspired step.

If your head feels foggy about what to do, ask. That's right. You can simply ask your inner guidance for the answer. Your job is to simply ask the question, "What is it that I need to do to align with my desire?" Then listen—to whatever answer you hear—just listen.

If no answer comes, relax. The answer may come later today. If it's your inner guidance answering, the dialogue will be short and sweet. It's easy to spot a message from your gremlin: the answers are often full of unnecessary details. Your gremlin likes to explain and justify at length. Ignore him and wait for cues from your inner guidance.

Exercise

In your Prosperity Journal, answer the following questions:

- What clues about my desire are being presented to me?
- What opportunities lay at my feet?
- What evidence can I see that things are unfolding perfectly for me?
- What one next step do I feel inspired to take?

Life Lesson #4
Relax Awhile and Allow

It's not how much you do, but how much love
you put into doing that matters.

Mother Teresa

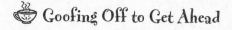

When you do the common things
in life in an uncommon way,
you will command the attention of the world.

GEORGE WASHINGTON CARVER

Four months into a new job as a 401(k) sales rep for a large national bank, management announced that if we didn't turn things around soon, all of us would be out of jobs. The whole department would have the plug pulled if we didn't create some impressive numbers fast.

Up until that time, we followed very prescribed steps for making a sale. We had to make a certain number of cold calls each day, set up a certain number of meetings each week, and use our list of responses to potential objections.

These were typical sales strategies that had been tried and proven many times for others. But it wasn't working for our sales team. The team was spending much of its time discussing what was going wrong, whose fault it was, and why things weren't working.

After learning our jobs were on the line if we didn't produce results pronto, I threw out my pipeline and script sheet and decided to try something else. Clearly, management's plan wasn't working.

I remembered hearing about a Pray Rain Journal. The theory was that if you wrote a page a day about what you wanted as if you already had it, by the time you got to the end of your book, you would have what you want. I didn't have a lot of time, so I pulled out the smallest book I could find—a two-by-three-inch notebook, about twenty-five pages long. It took all of two minutes to fill my first page.

I wrote about how excited prospects were to talk with me. How they loved our product and couldn't wait for me to implement it. I wrote about the instant excellent rapport we felt, and how the product we offered really was the perfect solution for their company.

After making my first entry, I checked in with myself about what felt good to do next.

Lunch!

I hadn't had a real lunch since my first week on the job, when upper management took me to the executive suite on my first day. My lunch "hour" since then had consisted of literally running down the hall to the vending machine. Then I would run back to my desk and eat my unhealthy fare between calls to business owners.

On this day, however, I decided on a better lunch. It felt truly luxurious to actually leave the building, sit at an outside table, and enjoy my favorite Greek food on a spring day. After I enjoyed a delicious meal, I kicked my feet up on the table and threw leftover pita bread to the sparrows nearby.

When I was good and ready, I meandered back to the office. I might have even been whistling. It was in the elevator, on the way back to my cubicle, that a stranger introduced himself to me and asked who I was. "I'm Jeannette, and I sell small business 401(k)s for the bank."

His jaw hit the floor. He couldn't believe his ears! He insisted I follow him to his office, which is where he showed me a desk littered with 401(k) sales literature from a variety of vendors.

He said he hadn't been able to make heads or tails of any of it, and had no idea my bank sold 401(k)s to small businesses. I shared my sales material. He was elated. It was exactly what he wanted. He asked how soon I could put this in place for his company.

In a bit of a daze, I let him introduce me to his Human Resources Director. He instructed the director to sign whatever I needed from her as soon as possible. He wanted this plan in place immediately!

End of the notebook? Within two hours of my first entry, I was already experiencing amazing success. My colleagues and manager were equally astounded. This never happened.

I attribute the happy result to giving up the "supposed to" actions management had given us, and instead doing what felt good. On that day for me, it meant imagining my success for just a few quick minutes, and taking a long lunch on a beautiful spring day with the birds.

Goofing off is highly underrated for creating life success!

Jeannette Maw

LIFE LESSON #4:
RELAX AWHILE AND ALLOW

Sometimes you just need a break. You may be forced to take a break because of an illness, lay-off, or some forced reason. Most of us take a break only when we are tired because we've been overdoing work, household stuff, running around, going to too many social events, or participating in sports. But there are other times when it is equally important to take a break.

What about taking a break from a goal? Have you had a particular goal on the list for what seems like forever? Give that goal a break! If you are not totally excited about a goal, give it a rest. Come back to the goal when it feels good to go for it. Otherwise, you're just "shoulding" all yourself.

It does not serve you to take action on something you are not inspired about. You may really want that goal, but you're ticked off about not manifesting it. Why make yourself wrong? That only increases the negative emotional charge and delays the manifestation of the desire.

We were very excited about writing this book, but the deadline to get the manuscript to our publisher was much shorter than anticipated. This meant that on top of the vacations and business trips we'd already scheduled, along with coaching sessions, workshops, and all the other details of running a business, we now had to devote an unexpected, heavy focus and time to the book project.

At times, the tight deadline was creating that knee-jerk reaction to *hurry up*. A decision was then made that we would indeed make the deadline—no matter what our current reality looked like. Once the decision was made to *stop pushing*—the flip side of *hurry up*—the Magic happened! One person on the team totally let go of the pressure to work on writing content; another embraced inspiration, sometimes cranking out an entire section in twenty-four hours. Another team member, who had scheduled a trip, committed to "letting go" of the book project for the time gone, knowing she would receive a welcoming e-mail upon her return. The "welcome back" e-mail, written by another team member, communicated the *collective download of inspiration* from our entire team.

Anytime members felt overwhelmed, another player would step up and remind them to *breathe*. Lots of e-mails and phone calls included conversations such as, "We'll get there. All is well. We're doing great! We're going to make the deadline!"

We asked the question: *What's the worst thing that could happen if we don't get it done on time?* The answer was usually nothing extreme or life-threatening.

Words to the Universe helped: *Universe, give us the perfect words to assist our readers in using the Law of Attraction to their highest benefit. Whatever we may fall behind with or can't get to, let someone else be able to handle joyfully. The more we relax, the better the book will be, and the more creativity will flow.*

And then we *breathed.* The more we remembered to breathe deeply, the connection with our collective inner guidance grew stronger—with every inhale, every exhale, every breath.

Exercise

Do you have a goal that gets put on your list every year, but you don't seem to do anything about it?

What if you took it off the list? That's right. Let it go. To keep seeing it there if you don't believe the situation is going to change is like a black cloud looming over your self-confidence. Wait until you are truly ready and excited to go for it.

Have you been trying to figure out something and the answer is not coming? Give it a rest! Chill out.

Let the answer find you when the time is right. You can't force a solution or an idea, but you can create the space for it.

You'll find that taking a break from anything is a good thing. Have you ever gotten out of your head and into your heart? That's a really great thing.

Choose to relax about one goal that you have been trying hard to manifest. Maybe the effort has been in your head and not in the doing. The desire that should have been here yesterday needs you to relax and allow it to manifest. Choose to put it on hold for a week. Relax about it. Let the Universe take over for a while.

How do you know when to stop resting? When it feels good to do so. You never need to be concerned about being inspired. There will always be an ebb and flow. You'll find yourself inspired for days, and then you may just want to relax with books and movies.

Trust that you will be inspired again. The timing of it all is none of your business. That's the job of the Universe. *If you feel inspired from a place of abundance to take action around it, go for it.*

Life Lesson #5
Trust "The" Voice

One new perception, one fresh thought,
one act of surrender,
one leap of faith
can change your life forever.

Robert Holden

How Two Dozen Eggs Hatched My Real-Estate Career

It was the Wednesday before Thanksgiving. I'd eaten lunch at the office, hoping to catch the FedEx lady as she made her rounds. I had tried to wait patiently, but every hour that passed took some of my patience with it.

As the sun began to retreat from the sky, the fading light dimmed my hopes. *I guess she's not going to come today, after all,* I thought to myself. I turned off the light and, just then, familiar footsteps began bounding up the steps and onto the porch. In another moment, she was inside. I ran out to greet her. "Do you have anything for me?" I could barely get out the words before she handed me the most wonderful envelope.

Inside was a signed listing agreement from a seller in Virginia. He had agreed to let me sell his home. This was my first listing. Delight filled my heart! *This house will sell this weekend, and it will sell for full price.*

Where on Earth did that thought come from? I quickly dismissed it, locked the door, and left.

On my way home, I stopped to place the sign in the yard and the lock box on the door. I stood back, wanting to remember this moment. I silently stared at the house, trying to burn it into my memory. *I was on my way!*

I spent Thanksgiving Day with my family, cell phone by my side, waiting for someone to call about the house. But no one did. *Well, it is Thanksgiving Day. It must be tomorrow that the call will come.*

Minutes after my arrival at work the next morning, my extension rang. The receptionist said that a gentleman was waiting in the lobby to speak with me about my listing. *Wow! This is great!* Turning the corner in the hallway, my smile vanished as I gazed upon the policeman. I glanced around the lobby, thinking surely there had been some mistake. Then the policeman shook my hand.

As soon as he spoke, I felt a chill well up from deep inside me. He asked, "Have you been by your listing this morning?"

"No, sir, I haven't been by the house," I said to the policeman. "I've just returned from visiting with my family."

My mind was racing, and none of my thoughts were good. Then, just as quickly, another quieter, calmer thought came: *This house will sell this weekend, and it will sell for full price.*

"I'm sorry," he said. "I don't have much time. The house was vandalized last night. It's pretty bad."

I couldn't imagine what had happened or why. When he asked if I had any idea who might be responsible, I shook my head, saying, "No, sir, I don't. I would like to help you, but I don't see how I can."

He handed me his card and started to leave. Looking back, he said, "Oh, you might want to call the seller so he can make some arrangements."

I grabbed my keys and headed for the house, unprepared for what I would find.

The dented mailbox greeted me with its lopsided grin. The mangled yard sign lay in the neighbor's yard. The contents of two trash cans blew across the yard. The damaged grill barely stood, and a large table from the deck above now lay in pieces on the ground. Sliced window screens waved in the wind, and bits of broken glass crunched underneath my feet.

Everything had been "egged." There was egg on the siding, on the decking, and on the driveway below. It smelled awful as it began to dry in the morning sun.

I wondered if I was cut out for this business. Maybe this was some kind of message. If this had happened on my first listing, I wondered what fun the tenth one might hold. Once again, the thought came to me: *This house will sell this weekend, and it will sell for full price.*

Yeah, right. For me, it was a disaster.

I got back in my car and put the key in the ignition. This was not in my job description. *I'll go back to the office, call the seller, and have him deal with it. After all, it is his house. I'll just get out and grab the sign so no one notices what happened to my listing.*

I backed out of the driveway and looked once more at the house. I don't know what made me pull back in, but I did.

That's when it hit me: this was *my* listing. The seller lived a state away. It was a holiday weekend on top of everything else. Then I made one of the best decisions of my life.

Although I really didn't want to, I chose to roll up my sleeves and pitch in. I cleaned the yard, picking up the trash and raking the front. Everything that had been dented, torn, and broken found a new home inside the storage shed. I popped out the dent from inside the mailbox. Then I cleaned off the sign, straightened it back into shape, and placed it in the front yard.

The broken glass presented a real problem. The window needed to be repaired quickly for security as well as protection in case of bad weather. Whom could I call? Then it came to me. Of course, I'd call Jim! Jim was friends with the owner of a local glass company. Within minutes, someone came over to repair the glass. Things were looking up.

Now only the egg remained. I hooked up a garden hose, and sprayed it all down—the siding, the decking, and the driveway. I found a scrub brush under the kitchen sink and began the hard work of scrubbing off the egg. I'd been at it for a little while when I heard a faint voice.

"Hello. Hello there," said an elderly lady who was walking her dog. She came closer. "Who are you, and what are you doing? I live nearby, and I've never seen you before."

Welcoming the chance to stand up straight, I rose to meet her. "Hi, I'm a real-estate agent. My name is Holleay, and this is my new listing. This morning a policeman informed me that the house had been vandalized. I thought I'd better get it cleaned up so it can sell this weekend."

The lady looked at me as if I had just landed from outer space. "You're a real-estate agent?" she asked. "I've never met an agent who would scrub down somebody's house."

"Well, I didn't know what else to do," I replied. "This house is going to sell this weekend. And it wouldn't have, not looking like this."

She asked for my number. I gave it to her, thinking nothing of it. Then I went back to finish the job.

The next day, my cell phone rang. It was the elderly lady. She said, "Do you remember me?" I said, "Of course, I enjoyed our chat. How may I help you?"

She started the conversation by saying that she didn't like real-estate agents. She'd been trying to sell her lot FSBO (for sale by owner) for months. She refused to list with any of the agents who had called her. She didn't trust them. But she figured she could trust an agent who was willing to scrub egg off a house to help it sell.

Our chance meeting produced several transactions. I sold the lady's house, helped her buy a new one, and sold that lot for her, too. She referred me to her friends, and I sold them a house. Several listings came from having my sign on her two properties. I also sold a number of homes to buyers who called in after seeing those two signs. Many of them became repeat clients who bought and sold with me for several years.

The seemingly chance meeting with a woman walking her dog proved to be a wave that washed over me time and time again, bringing me even more clients and commissions. To think that my real-estate career had been hatched by two dozen eggs!

Looking back, I often wonder what I would have missed if I'd simply called the seller instead of scrubbing off those eggs. I'm so glad I chose to listen to my intuition instead. Oh, yes, just in case you were wondering, the house did indeed sell that very weekend. And for *full price*!

Holleay Parcker

LIFE LESSON #5:
TRUST "THE" VOICE

Have you ever felt that a decision to take action propels you in a direction least expected? You find yourself saying yes or no to something that you would have bet against yourself saying the day before in a similar situation? Yet, there you are, taking action with all your heart, and enjoying the process. What is *that* all about?

Inspired actions and allowing yourself to manifest a desire go hand in hand. It's the easy road. Inspired actions are like stepping-stones on the path of your life's dreams. One step leads to the next. You can take small, medium, or giant steps depending on your mood. Often, you will take an action that seems simply like the smart decision in that moment. You might call it a no-brainer.

For example, a woman wants a new couch; she has wanted it for a while. She has her mental checklist of all the qualities her perfect couch must own. She walks downtown to meet a colleague for lunch, and she spies *the couch* in the window of a furniture store. She takes a detour into the store and finds a sale sign on her perfect couch for the perfect price. She'd had the money set aside for this exact moment. Sold!

In our example, you'd think the woman was crazy if she didn't purchase her perfect couch. It seemed like the logical thing to do, right? Yet, many people don't listen to the voice that says, "Go for it."

Have you ever had an idea for a business or an urge to connect with someone you admire but then talked yourself out of it? Or what about that vacation you've been talking about for years? Then the voice that gives you the grand idea gets cancelled out by some other voice.

And then more voices chime in. Remember those gremlins we talked about previously? It's very easy to blow off an idea or decision when there is a committee in your head voting against it. Many times there is a committee around you in real life talking about all the reasons you should or shouldn't do something, too. If someone gives you their negative feedback, that is their own gremlin talking, not yours. Suggestions are welcome, but always follow what brings you joy and feels right in your gut.

You are free to choose who and what you listen to. Your inner guidance system will always point you in the direction of what is in your highest good. The sooner you listen, the quicker the joy. Your inner guidance voice can be trusted. It will never let you down.

Inspired ideas and actions are handed over from Spirit. The moment the idea pops in your brain, it's a green light to go from the Universe. You can't have an idea or desire without the ability and resources to manifest it. That is law.

The only things that get in the way are your thoughts and then lack of action. If you listen to all the negative chatter about why it won't work out for you, you'll stay in the same place you've always been.

Yes, sometimes the action you take will seem like a knee-jerk reaction without back-up guarantees. That's perfectly fine. Other times you'll do some research to aid you in moving forward. When following these impulses, it will feel grounded and not chaotic, although you may still feel like you're jumping out of a plane with no prior experience. That's okay.

Following inspiration is the key to having amazing experiences and manifesting joy on a daily basis. The icing on the cake will be that you will be prosperous as a result.

Exercise

In your Prosperity Journal, write down two to three times in the past when you got an inspired idea and acted on it. What was the outcome? Now write down two to three times in the past when you got an inspired idea, but your gremlin kicked in and you did not act on it. What was the outcome? Today, be aware of your intuition and ideas that come to you and be willing to take inspired action. When an idea sparks or you feel guided to do something, follow it. Be curious.

Essential Ingredient #5

BABY STEPS LEAD
TO AVALANCHES

*Most great people have attained
their greatest success just one step
beyond their greatest failure.*

Napoleon Hill

off the mark.com   by Mark Parisi

ATLANTIC FEATURE © 1992 MARK PARISI

CATNIP 50lb

CATN 50lbs

50lbs

JEEPERS... MY BIRTHDAY HAS BEEN PRETTY UNEVENTFUL SO FAR

offthemark.com

MARK PARISI

Life Lesson #1
The Power of a Single Step

· ·

Life affords no higher pleasure than that of
surmounting difficulties, passing from one
step of success to another, forming new
wishes and seeing them gratified.

Samuel Johnson

☕ A Poor Village Boy's Journey to the American Dream

I do not think there is any other quality
so essential to success of any kind
as the quality of perseverance.
It overcomes almost everything, even nature.

JOHN D. ROCKEFELLER

I stopped by the ice-cream truck and said, "Sir, direction please." The man looked at me and yelled, "Speak English. Speak English!" But the more I dug in my memory for some mismatched words to make up a sentence, the more impatient he became. Maybe he was losing a sale or two because of my interruption. I stopped trying, gave up, and walked away.

It had only been a short eight months since I arrived in America. I was twenty years old. My personal possessions were five dollars, two shirts, and one pair of pants, and I didn't speak any English. A scary thought entered my mind. *How will I ever make it in this country if I cannot communicate what I am thinking?*

Some people assumed I was not intelligent because I didn't speak English. Since I could not prove them wrong, I needed to do something about it. While many were on the path to success, I was on the path to learning just enough to get by.

Since I was not qualified for any work in America, I settled for menial labor. Even a fast-food restaurant turned me down for a job to pick up trash in the parking lot. To this day, I'm not sure if the trash cans would have had a hard time understanding me.

After so many attempts at trying to get a job only to hear that my English was not good enough, I settled for anything. I begged a boat carpenter to let me be his helper.

"Sir, I'm a fast learner," I said to him. He gave me my first part-time job. I washed cars on the street for five and six dollars a pop, mopped floors, and dug holes in between.

The pay was not great, but it afforded me a much better life than the one I'd had as a sick child in an impoverished village in Haiti. At least I was no longer struggling with hunger, poverty, and diseases. More importantly, I was no longer sleeping on a dirt floor with rats and roaches crossing over me at night, occasionally nibbling the bottoms of my feet.

All along, I continued to learn English. Every day I wrote three words on my hand and committed them to memory. In the meantime, I was hearing about the American Dream. It was talked about on television, in newspapers, and everyday conversations.

Twenty-three years ago, it seemed as though more people believed in the dream. Now, it is hardly mentioned. During my struggling years in this country, there was never any doubt in my mind that the American Dream was alive. There's plenty of evidence suggesting that one can live an abundant life in this country.

I had some ideas about what it would take to succeed in America. Going the extra mile, resilience, persistence, and hard work were at the top of my list. But the road to success requires a lot more than that. It requires specific know-how. Being persistent without a combination of street and book smarts is a delusion.

My work was cut out for me. It would be a long time before I would be able to pick up a book and understand what was in it. So, what did I do to go from where I was to where I am today? The answer is a lot of preparation. Abraham Lincoln said, "I shall study and prepare myself. Someday, my chance will come."

The first order of things for me was to learn English. I invested in a tiny dictionary, and bought a couple of children's books so I could see the pictures and the words at the same time. Every day, I continued to write three words on my hand. At the end of each week, I reviewed my words.

Once I knew enough words, I needed to learn how to pronounce them so that others could understand me. Having to keep repeating myself over and over again was somewhat humiliating and embarrassing. God bless whoever invented tongue twisters. I bought a book and twisted my tongue until it hurt. In case you don't know, the tongue is a lazy muscle in the body. Just like most people, it prefers to stay in a comfortable position.

In my case, I had been speaking Creole for twenty-one years. It's the position that my tongue knew and felt comfortable with. Forcing it to speak English was torture. My mind was speaking English, but my tongue was speaking Creole. That caused me to have a hard-to-understand accent. It's the reason why most new immigrants' accents sound so different. Fortunately, I worked day and night to retrain my tongue.

After spinning my wheels trying to make ends meet as a broke immigrant in Miami, Florida, I moved to Atlanta, Georgia. There I landed a job as a doorman at an upscale hotel: the Waverly Renaissance Hotel.

To some degree, the doorman job was my entrée to a life of abundance. It wasn't because I was rolling in dough, but because of the education it afforded me. In life, it's not what we have and the position we occupy that matters. It's the person we are becoming. It's the courage to travel an extra mile and do what most are not willing to do.

While parking cars at the hotel, I discovered which books were being read by the people who looked like they were living the American Dream. I made it a habit to constantly scan the back seats for self-improvement books and tapes. I bought everything I saw.

I devoured every book and listened to every tape over

and over. In no time, my brain was saturated with "you-can-do-it messages." I felt unstoppable. I wrote down my goals and the plans to achieve them. One of my goals was to speak on platforms across the country. Although some people either directly or indirectly suggested I could not achieve that goal, I dared to believe I could.

My supervisor told me that no one would ever pay me to speak. He cited several reasons, including the fact that I was a foreigner and my English was horrible. And, of course, there were the friends and family members who wondered what career I would choose while speaking on platforms.

"Hi, sir, I'm Rene Godefroy . . . your doorman. My dream is to become a speaker just like you one day." I said these words to Dan Burrus, Jeffrey Gitomer, and several other speakers I met at the door. Dan and Jeffrey are big names in the industry. To my surprise, they both took the time to give advice. It was such a breath of fresh air to see that there are people out there who build and inspire hope in others.

I knew it would be hard to reconnect with those heavy hitters in the speaking industry. They are busy, and their gatekeepers are vigilant. Once I learned that they were members of the National Speakers Association (NSA), I immediately set a goal to attend a convention. Of course, money was tight, but my determination was huge. It is often said that you can tell the size of someone's commitment by watching where he or she spends their money and time.

I saved my tip money for the convention. Off I went. When you are in a room full of almost 2000 people, it can be overwhelming. But I wanted to speak with Jeffrey, Dan, and the others I had met at the door.

I reintroduced myself to them. "Hi, sir, I'm Rene Godefroy . . . your doorman from Atlanta. I told you I was going to be a speaker. Here I am." Jeffrey gave me a big squeeze and introduced me to several other high-powered speakers.

Dan Burrus pulled me into a corner. "I want you to keep coming back again and again," he said. "I can feel the fire in your belly. You are definitely going to make it." He also gave me a list of things to do. I did all of them.

In a few short years, the board of NSA heard my story. Somehow I got selected to speak at one of the conventions in a general session. The rest is history.

I was discovered by speakers' bureaus and meeting planners. Jeffrey Gitomer wrote the foreword for my book, *Kick Your Excuses Good-bye*. Today, I am living the good life I dreamed about and worked so hard for. I travel this great land of plenty helping others embrace the changes that are going on in their personal and professional lives. Resisting change creates atrophy instead of growth and progress.

Abundance and the American Dream are accessible to anyone in this country. The only thing that may be between you and your dream are your excuses and the limitations you place on yourself. Some people really fight to hold on to their excuses. They curse their luck, instead of expressing gratitude for the opportunities that are available to them.

My aim is to inspire hope and encourage others. Hopefully, I have done just that for you. Please never, ever, ever give up. Dare to go an extra mile in everything you do. True abundance and success are patiently waiting for you on the extra mile.

Press on!

Rene Godefroy

LIFE LESSON #1:
THE POWER OF A SINGLE STEP

Have you learned from the lessons that everyday life has tossed out? Do you look at what life has to offer as challenges, but approach them as opportunities? If so, we would wager that you do learn from your experiences. On the other hand, if you are more apt to place blame on yourself or others, use excuses to explain a circumstance, or prefer to be a spectator in life, then you are probably missing out on some wonderful opportunities!

It isn't necessary for you to accept the blame for everything that occurs in life. But just because you don't accept the blame does not mean that you can assign it to someone else. Why give them the control over a situation? Things happen, but it is up to each of us to use these things to our advantage whenever possible and take charge of our lives. By taking one step at a time, it is our responsibility to use whatever tools are at our disposal to achieve the goals we set—no matter what the obstacle.

Consider this scenario: Cindy has led a tough life. She left home at a young age and lived on the streets, yet she still managed to make the most of her life. She went to college, earned several degrees, and has a successful career in banking. Cindy *did* learn the lessons of life and paid attention . . . unlike Andrew. Andrew also did not have an easy time of it while he was growing up, but instead of allowing his circumstances to fuel his desire to achieve and succeed, he allowed them to limit him. He focused on how rough his young life was, how unfairly he'd been treated, and how much he was owed due to his wronged past. Andrew has not found success. In fact, just when things look like they are about to turn around for him, Andrew's attitude becomes a weapon of self-sabotage. He has thoroughly mastered the art of laying blame, but not the lesson of accepting responsibility for oneself and taking the steps necessary to create success. Andrew, for now, seems quite comfortable living his life at the ends of a puppeteer's strings instead of taking responsibility and controlling his own destiny. Have you ever noticed how two people raised in the same house, with the same influences, sometimes react so differently to similar situations?

How do you react to the things that life dishes out? If you find yourself wondering how you made it to this point in your life, or you are questioning how to get to a different point, just ask yourself if you've been the driver or the passenger thus far. There is a saying, "There is no such thing as an accident." The things that occur in life do not just happen. You have the power to control your life by accepting responsibility for what shows up, and using each experience as a learning tool.

Exercise

1. Take out your Prosperity Journal and draw a line down the middle of the page. In the left-hand column, list the areas in your life where you feel challenged. In the right-hand column, identify the opportunity within each challenge.
2. Next, for each opportunity, identify one step you can take now toward the opportunity you've identified.
3. Then decide when you will take that step. Put that date next to your action step. One next step is all you need to get the momentum going.
4. Now, as Nike says, "Just do it!"
5. Once you've taken that step, identify what your next step will be. Set the date by which you'll have taken your next step and resolve to go for it.
6. Repeat steps two through five as often as necessary.

Life Lesson #2
The Power of Being
100 Percent Responsible

Success is failure with the dirt brushed off.

Mamie McCullough

☕ Success in the Face of Adversity

Love isn't love till you share it with others.

ANONYMOUS

I started stuttering when I was four and a half years old. It would sometimes take me several minutes just to say my own name. Some experts said my stuttering was a result of being lost in a forest while out on a day trip with my parents. During a picnic, I had wandered off from my parents and ended up lost for many hours before being found. That traumatic experience, the catalyst for my stuttering, would affect my life for the next thirty years.

I felt inferior to other people, always trying to overcompensate because of my stuttering, wanting to please other people, to be liked and accepted. I guess today you would call that low self-esteem, a lack of confidence. Growing up, I felt I missed out on so much because of my stuttering, suffering much rejection and ridicule because of it. Kids at school were tough on me, and teachers ignored my hand when I tried to answer questions in class. Later, job interviews challenged me.

I eventually took a job as an apprentice hairdresser because it seemed like a job where speaking would not be a prerequisite, and I went on to become a successful hairdresser, training at the world-famous Vidal Sassoon Company.

My time at Sassoon was very exciting; I learned so much there, not just about hairdressing, but about life and serving others. I also had the opportunity to meet the great Vidal Sassoon himself, who made a lasting impression on me. My speech even improved because I became more confident; it wasn't perfect, but at least I could communicate. The people at Vidal Sassoon were the first to see beyond my disability and were willing to give me a chance to prove myself.

I went on to open my own hair salons, and just when things seemed to be going so well, I had a relapse in my speech. It was the worst it had been since I was at school. I could not control it, no matter how hard I tried. The setback was devastating for me. I realized that drastic action was needed. I finally had to take responsibility for my speech and for doing something about it.

Ironically, around that time I was channel surfing on the television and came across an exposé about a man in Scotland with an alternative approach to stuttering. After several attempts, booking the course and then canceling, I finally found the determination to go.

In 1986, I enrolled in the one-week intensive speech course in Scotland. I remember standing in line at Manchester's Victoria Train Station on a cold Sunday morning waiting to purchase my ticket to Edinburgh, Scotland. As I approached the ticket agent, I tried to give him my destination, but no words would come out. I was paralyzed with fear. My head shook from side to side in an attempt to get out my words. People behind me were getting impatient, so I took a piece of paper from my case and wrote down what I could not say, and then handed it to the agent.

I promised myself then and there that I would never allow myself to be humiliated like that again. In that moment, I knew there was no going back for me. I would succeed in overcoming my stuttering no matter what it took. I had struggled with speech all my life, but to be fair and really honest, I had lacked the courage to do something about it. I kept waiting for someone to come along with that magic bullet—an instant fix that would make everything right. To this day, I keep that note I wrote to the ticket agent as a reminder of the past.

The course was run like a boot camp, but the methods worked. Total discipline and commitment were required. At the end of the course, although I was speaking very slowly, I was not stuttering for the first time in over thirty years. My confidence was sky high, and I had new hope for the future, but I was under no illusions about the task ahead. I knew old habits died hard, and I was going to need all my resolve and discipline to use the techniques I was taught, and to do the two hours of practice required each day to reinforce my new way of speaking and thinking. I enlisted the support of family and friends to help and encourage me along the way. This network of people helped me tremendously.

It took me three years to learn how to use my new voice and find my comfort level. There were setbacks along the way, but I was determined to maintain my fluency and succeed. I refused to let these setbacks defeat me, as they would have done in the past.

To challenge myself further, I went on to a new career in sales, working my way up from sales representative with my company to National Sales Manager within eighteen months. I tripled sales in my territory and earned several prestigious awards.

Many years ago, when I was on my way to that speech course, I set myself the goal of one day speaking in public. I used to close my eyes and imagine myself on stage, speaking in a way I could only dream about, looking at the smiling faces in front of me, and hearing the warm round of applause from the audience. I never let go of that dream.

Today, I am living my dream. I am president of my own successful company and fortunate to make my living as a highly sought-after professional speaker, sharing my message and story with audiences worldwide. Ironically, my voice and my speech—once my greatest fear and enemy— have now become my best friends.

I look back at my struggle with speech in a strange way as a blessing. It has taught me to be more tolerant and respectful of other people with differences, and it has made me very grateful and appreciative of everything I have in life. I take nothing for granted. I say to people, "Whatever challenges you are facing, you can overcome them. The only limitations are those you impose on yourself. Believe in yourself, find your inner strength, have courage, be 100 percent committed. Take full responsibility for your life, surround yourself with positive, supportive people, and dream big, big dreams. They really do come true."

Charles Marcus

Life Lesson #2:
The Power of Being 100 Percent Responsible

Do you wish that you could do something over, take back an action, or exchange an utterance? The bad news is that you can't—what's done is done. The good news is that it's already in the past, and this is the first moment of the rest of your life. Since you can't change the past, what does your future hold? It's up to you to choose.

As a society, we often get stuck in ruts. Not satisfied with our past and our present, but reluctant to step up to the plate and make the future we desire, we don't realize that we created the path we are on consciously or unconsciously. But nothing is written in stone. Change begins first with a thought, followed by a choice, which becomes an action.

Are there things in your life that you would like to release? Or things that you would like to see materialize? Are you ready to make the choice to *be* what you want?

Close your eyes and visualize your dream life. If it's different from the life you have, then you have a choice to make. Become aware of the thoughts that you hold. Simply by changing them to thoughts of appreciation will have a profound effect on your life. Don't worry about what has already happened. Remember, this is the *first moment* of the rest of your life.

When you decide to take 100 percent responsibility for your life, it means you no longer make excuses or play victim. It means you choose to let go of the Complain and Blame Game. You acknowledge that everything that happens to you is of your doing, whether wanted or not.

The choices you make from moment to moment determine your results. It's up to you to decide to think differently and behave differently in order to achieve *different* results.

Exercise

1. Get out your Prosperity Journal and write at the top of the page, "How did I create this issue in my life?" Notice this isn't a list of how someone else created the problem. The question releases all blame and victimhood. This is your opportunity to identify your role in creating the situation. What were the choices you made, the perspectives you held, the things you said or didn't say, the assumptions you made? You are taking 100 percent responsibility for having this issue or situation in your life.

2. At the top of the next page in your Journal write, "What can I do to resolve the issue?" This is your opportunity to focus on what you do want, putting your energy and attention on the results you'd like to experience. Again, you are taking 100 percent responsibility for your life.

3. From your list of answers in Step 2, determine your next action and take it.

4. When setbacks occur, remember to hold your focus on your intended outcome and ask, "What can I do to resolve this?" and get back into action.

5. Be sure to congratulate yourself for taking back control of your life!

Life Lesson #3
Pay It Forward and Create Miracles

There are only two ways to live your life.
One is as though nothing is a miracle.
The other is as though everything is a miracle.

Albert Einstein

☕ Dave's Legacy: The Miracle of Giving

Love never reasons, but profusely gives—gives
like a thoughtless prodigal, its all—and
trembles then lest it has done too little.

HANNAH MOORE

My life and business are based on the simple principles of the Law of Attraction. I attribute my success in health, business, and relationships to the power of belief, intention, energy, and focus . . . and to having fun. I believe what Abraham-Hick's publication teaches . . . that the basis of our lives is freedom, and the object of our lives is joy.

As I've learned to practice and implement the Law of Attraction, I've manifested some wonderful things in the past two years: achieved the number-twelve position in a young network-marketing company, earned a deluxe cruise to the Caribbean and a week-long all-expenses-paid trip to a five-star resort in Maui, won a $2,000 monster gas grill (my husband's in heaven), and (saving the best for last) won a brand-new 2005 PT Convertible Cruiser.

Life was grand, and my family and I were really cruising. Then, on January 3, 2006, we learned that my youngest brother Dave's lung cancer had returned. Because of my success in network marketing, I had both the financial means and the time to travel to Florida and be with Dave. During this time, a good friend sent me a card and asked if she could add Dave and his wife, Diane, to a "Blessing Circle." I was deeply touched, and, of course, I said yes.

During the next eight months, Dave received hundreds of cards. People we had never met sent us cards. Dave loved and cherished every card he received. He told me, with tears in his eyes and a huge smile on his face, that the cards encouraged and inspired him to continue living with hope and expressing his love to those around him on a daily basis.

When I went to Florida to visit Dave for the last time, I counted more than a hundred cards taped to his wall with another two-hundred-plus cards in his closet. I called the wall "Dave's Wall of Love" and the senders of his cards "Dave's Angels."

Dave died on September 11, 2006, at the age of forty-six. I was deeply saddened by his death and missed him tremendously. I was also angry and disappointed at my father. I felt my father had not been there for Dave in his time of need. I didn't like the resentment and disappointment that seemed to have a grip on me, but I didn't know how to shake it.

Then I had an inspired thought. I remembered Dave's Angels and his Wall of Love. *If I want to be filled with love, joy, and forgiveness, I should send a card.* And so I created a wonderful tribute to Dave and sent it to all of his angels.

I felt an immediate ease and lightness, as though a weight had been lifted from my heart. Not only had I paid tribute to Dave, but I had transitioned to a place of love and appreciation.

However, my heart wasn't completely joyful. I still harbored residual feelings of hurt, anger, disappointment, and frustration toward my father. And then it dawned on me—*send him cards*. So, I did, and a remarkable thing happened. The more cards I sent, the better I felt, and the more love I experienced for my father. I completely healed my relationship with him with one simple act—repeatedly sending him cards of love, appreciation, and acknowledgement. And, in the process, he became more light-hearted, fun, kinder, and loving to me. I experienced total lightness of being.

Clearly, the love and support our family received as a result of this experience has had a major impact on both my business and me. Of course, the daily practice of sending cards is truly a wonderful way to celebrate, to acknowledge people, and to stay in touch, and this has always been a goal of mine, but there are many unexpected rewards as well.

Sending cards has definitely had a positive impact on my business. I attract and retain more loyal customers and distributors, and I receive more referrals. My income is increasing, and I am having so much more fun. I feel rejuvenated and inspired. I have truly learned what it is to work and serve with love. I have learned to focus on the positive aspects of everyone and everything, and it has been truly amazing to watch as more miracles occur. This is Dave's legacy to me, and it is rippling through the lives of everyone I meet. As more of us become senders of cards, we become more loving, more appreciative, more forgiving, and—surprise, surprise—more prosperous.

I thought by sending out cards that I would be enriching and inspiring other people. The wonderful side benefit is how sending out cards has enriched and inspired my life. How cool is that?

Barb Gau, MSW, LCSW

LIFE LESSON #3:
PAY IT FORWARD AND CREATE MIRACLES

What if there was a way you could maximize the potential that you could be helping someone nearly every day? There is a way that you can make it happen—by paying it forward. You may have seen the movie *Pay It Forward*.

Paying it forward is the opposite of paying it back.

When someone does you a favor, what do you typically say? "Thanks so much. I'll pay you back." Instead of paying it back, do something nice for someone else. Only instead of paying it forward once, do it twice. Thus, one good deed could spawn hundreds of others in a relatively short time as you ask others to pay it forward instead of paying you back.

Trevor, the twelve-year-old hero of the movie *Pay It Forward*, thinks of quite an idea. He describes it to his mother and teacher as doing a good deed for three people. These three people then do a good deed for someone else instead of returning the favor to him. This grows exponentially. It begins with three and then those three become nine and so on. Pretty soon hundreds of people are doing favors and paying it forward.

The "Pay It Forward" concept of doing unselfish acts of kindness, a service for someone, and then asking them to pay the kindness forward instead of paying it back is a powerful idea.

So when you do someone a favor, ask them to pay it forward.

Exercise:

1. Look for an opportunity this week to do an unselfish act of kindness for someone and ask them to pay the kindness forward to someone else.
2. In your Prosperity Journal, write about what the experience was like for you and how it made you feel.
3. From now on, whenever someone does something nice for you, look for two opportunities to pay it forward.

Be prepared to sit back and watch the rippling effect of how powerful and positive this is. It will help make this year a better year for many . . . as well as for you!

Life Lesson #4
How to Make Fear Your Ally

Our greatest glory is not in never falling,
but in rising every time we fall.

Confucius

☕ Somebody Give Me a Hand

Do or do not . . . there is no try.

I teach, write, and coach about prosperity, and yet I was up to my ears in debt. *Argh!* I was stumbling to walk-my-talk, and all my attention was on what I *didn't* want. I didn't want that debt, and I didn't want to be constantly harassed by my former mate. My power felt like a thing of distant memories.

I kept searching for my old creativity and enthusiasm, but the more I pushed for it, the more it eluded me. Two years earlier, I had been debt-free. I had just sold my house, paid off everything but my car, and was ready to create a new life.

My reality now was very far from what I desired. Now I just wanted someone to come and whisk away all my troubles. My laptop had been stolen from my office, my car tires had been flattened, my BMW had been sprayed with acid, up to sixty messages a day were being left on my phone by a hurt and angry male, and my wallet and cell phone had been stolen out of my car. I was feeling victimized, and found myself constantly looking around every corner for what might happen next.

After a year of what felt like insanity, I finally realized the only one who could help me was myself. My family and friends were very supportive, but I was the one who had to shift my focus. I had spent a lot of time trying to figure out what I needed to do to get it back together. But it got worse before it got better, and I was very hard on myself about why I had let my life slide into such a dark place. I had created my own private hell.

The intensity of my emotions felt like a vapor lock. I needed some serious help. Another coach friend recommended a spiritual coach. Week in and week out, she helped me let go of my constant fear-based mind games. Even though I hired her, I thought she might fire me. I felt like a child, going over the same issues every week. The coach hung in there with me for eight months, assisting me with keeping the faith so that I would see the light again. She and my business partner, Eva, both pointed out every inch of progress I made, even when I couldn't see it.

Several months into my transformation, my new mate pointed out that I was still not making any changes with my business. His words stung, but he was right. I was doing what I loved, but I hadn't decided to step back into the energetic and passionate person I once was. My income was keeping me afloat, but I wasn't attracting the profits that I had in the past. I had just enough money to make minimum payments on my high credit-card bills, and I seemed to be in a holding pattern. I decided to get a grip on my wealth.

That week I faced the numbers. Instead of complaining about my finances, it was time to see exactly what was going on. I ran Quickbooks reports and made spreadsheets. The reality wasn't pretty. I rolled up my sleeves and made a plan on paper. I would pay off my boat first by making bigger payments. It was the smallest balance in the debt column. I decided it would feel best to make just above minimum payments on everything else. I gave myself a target date of a year to completely pay down all debt. It seemed so far away, and I had no idea how I was going to increase my income to execute this plan.

Two months into my mission, my passion was back in full swing. I felt empowered that I had taken action, although smaller than I had wanted, to move my finances into a state of abundance. I found a savings account I had forgotten about and used that money to pay off the boat. Yes! Next on the plan was paying off a line of credit. A couple of months later, it was gone, too. This game was getting to be fun! I appreciated every dollar that I was paying toward my bills. The momentum was driving up my spirits.

Within eight months, I had doubled my income, and all but one debt remained unpaid. And I was not doing anything different in terms of marketing or changing business systems. I was just very clear that I was going to surpass my highest income-grossing year. I was done suffering. I knew what I was capable of regarding wealth, joy, peace, and fulfillment. The more excited I got, the more business I attracted.

One of the best things that transpired during this time was that the relationship with my new mate took a positive turn. A feeling of trust, security, and partnership began to fill my heart, and it continues to do so. Although the road getting here took some time, the foundation I've built is stronger than it has ever been. I consistently look back on those times and know my trust in the Law of Attraction is unwavering. I can be and do anything!

Jeanna Gabellini

LIFE LESSON #4: HOW TO MAKE FEAR YOUR ALLY

It is human nature to try to control the various aspects of life, yet fear is often allowed to wrest the control away. Why give anything that kind of power over your life? Isn't it time to stop letting fear hinder you from doing, being, or achieving what you desire? When fear is holding you back from what you really want, it is time to face it head-on and move through it. How can fear be overcome? It is not as difficult as it may initially look.

First, please realize that FEAR is nothing more than False Evidence Appearing Real. Knowing that it is false is the key that shifts the power back to you and puts the ball back in your court. The thing that moves you to take action brings your fear to light and causes its power to dissipate. Confidence is built up, and the fear is transformed into excitement, which brings you that much closer to success.

Exercise

Get out your Prosperity Journal and utilize these five baby steps to cross the barrier from fearful to fearless:

1. Identify your fear or fears. Make sure you are aware of the entire situation. It is not uncommon for more than one fear to be at the root of a problem, or a fear from long ago resurfacing to couple with a new one.
2. Identify what is holding you back from being, doing, or having whatever you desire. You need a clear understanding of what must be overcome in order for you to successfully combat it.
3. Identify what you would do if you didn't have that fear. Visualize what your life would be like if this albatross did not exist. How would you feel? How many more opportunities would be available to

you? How many more adventures would exist? How much happier would you be?

4. Identify situations when you faced fear and successfully moved beyond it. With a little thought, everyone can identify situations where they moved beyond fear to reach a desired outcome (a new relationship, a new job, graduation, a wedding, and more). This can be any situation in which you faced your dragon and triumphed. Use these times as touchstones you carry in your pocket to remind you that you can do this again.

5. Identify the qualities in you that helped you succeed. These qualities are the foundation for your success and, typically, the foundation for you as a person—tenacity, integrity, zeal, confidence, being able to see the big picture, to name a few.

So, how are you letting your fears stop you? How can you take the Pause button off of *your* life? What are some of the qualities that you have drawn upon in the past to overcome your fears and reach your dreams? Now is the time. Seize control of your life again.

Life Lesson #5
Close Your Eyes and Dream

Dreams are powerful reflections
of your actual growth potential.

Denis Waitley and Reni L. Witt, The Joy of Working

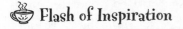
Flash of Inspiration

Dreaming illustrates your hidden
capacities and your unawakened ability.

PETER DANIELS

Life can change in an instant. Sometimes it just takes a while for that instant to arrive.

I had put my son in his stroller and headed down to the hiking trail that surrounds Austin's Town Lake. The five-mile walk around that section of the lake had become my daily ritual. I loved watching the rowers glide across the water as the sun rose higher in the eastern sky. I loved the backdrop provided by the tall buildings downtown, and the subdued hum of traffic on the bridges. Even now, at the beginning of autumn, I could smell newly mown grass and follow along pathways sheltered by tall, deep green foliage. An occasional fisherman would look up from his place on the shore and wave good morning. From time to time, Matthew would extend his little arms and call out to birds searching for their breakfast.

My time was my own now. A year and a half earlier, I had left my job in a public agency to open my own consulting business. I had been writing grants for years, and with my expertise in affordable housing, I soon had a few clients. Among them was the developer of an apartment complex for senior citizens. I was excited about the project, and enjoying the challenge of helping the developer put it together and convincing the city government to provide funding. Because I believed in the project, I accepted minimal upfront compensation, with the rest of my fee contingent on securing the grant we were seeking.

Money was not pouring in, but I was making a living. I had a group of wonderful friends, a comfortable apartment, and a dependable car. I had been devastated when Matthew's father left before he was born, but I was recovering and building a life on my own terms.

Matt is my "second family." Twenty years earlier, I had been a single mother with two small children, and life had been a constant struggle. It took me years of part-time classes to finish my degree. Even working two and sometimes three jobs at a time, I barely kept food on the table. I can't remember how often we lived without a phone, lights, or heat. Worst of all, I never seemed to have enough time to just enjoy my older son and daughter. I was often deeply depressed, and only my devotion to my children kept me moving forward.

During those twenty years, however, I began what has been a lifetime of spiritual study. I started writing down my vision of the life I desired. I made "treasure maps" with pictures cut out of magazines. I trained myself to focus on the aspects of my life for which I was grateful, and not to dwell on my troubles. The results were gradual. I hadn't experienced a dramatic change in my circumstances. It was more as though I had been gradually ascending a staircase, with each step bringing me to a happier, more prosperous level.

That day, walking around the lake, I was thinking of the various challenges presented by the senior housing project, and the ways I was going to overcome each one. I'm a project person, and my creative juices were flowing. Perhaps it was a confluence of the exercise endorphins, glorious nature all around me, and the creative high that generated the perfect moment for that flash of inspiration. I only know that suddenly, with an almost physical force, an idea came into my head.

I could create a housing project for single parents and their families, and I could get a grant to make it happen.

The idea was so stunning, and so completely new and unexpected, I had to sit down on a nearby bench. I was literally unable to stay on my feet. Thoughts began swirling in my mind. Throughout my professional life, I had worked with women and children, and I knew firsthand the difficulties faced by low-income single parents. I was a counselor, and I understood how to provide social services. I was the correct person to do this project. And, most importantly, I knew how to get it funded.

After that, things began to move quickly. I found an apartment complex in foreclosure and convinced the bank that owned it to accept $500 earnest money for a long-term option on the property. I found a contractor who agreed do the necessary renovations. I stayed up all night for weeks at a time, developing plans and writing financial projections. During the final couple of months before the funding decision was made, I started running out of money and even applied for food stamps.

I was obsessively devoting myself to a single endeavor, working with tunnel vision. To some of my friends and family, it looked as though I had stepped off that staircase to prosperity. They worried I was putting all my eggs in a single basket, and wondered what would happen to me if the funding was denied.

After six long months of hard work, the day of decision arrived. I sat in City Council chambers, waiting for the vote that would decide my future. Several hours passed as council members discussed road development and benefits for city employees—important issues, of course, but not the reasons I was sitting in that audience, my hands clasped tightly together to hold them still.

Finally, the mayor looked down at the agenda and began to read the names of the proposed affordable housing projects. The first two were approved. Two others failed. Then he requested a vote on my client's senior housing project. Yes, it passed!

I was grateful, but still shaking with anticipation. I couldn't help wondering, *What if my project was not approved? Where would I go in my life? Would I lose my one big chance to have the future I had dreamed of, the one I'd written about in my journal, the one I affirmed to myself every day?*

Then I heard the mayor ask for a vote on Friendship Place Apartments. One by one, the council members responded, then the mayor added his own, "Aye." By a unanimous vote, my project was approved.

A few weeks later, I had a check in my hand: a 100 percent grant to close the purchase and pay for all the remodeling.

I owned Friendship Place for eight years. During that time, we served several hundred low-income families. We provided a childcare center, counseling groups, and referrals to job training. I was able to spend time with Matthew, while helping other mothers and children.

Of course, I moved much further up that staircase of abundance. I eventually married a wonderful man, and today we have a beautiful home and a joyful family life. We work for ourselves, and we travel and do the things we have both always wanted to do.

Prosperity is a process of asking for and believing in and accepting our good. For most of us, prosperity does not happen all at once. What often does happen in an instant, when we're ready, is that flash of Divine inspiration. Then it is up to us to take inspired action.

Jillian Coleman Wheeler

LIFE LESSON #5:
CLOSE YOUR EYES AND DREAM

The dreams you hold in your heart can shape your reality if you take the time to give them life . . . to visualize them. Do you ever wonder about the self-confidence that successful people always seem to have? It's that self-confidence that got them where they wanted to be. They focused on the goal, and the mind and body made it happen.

Exercise

In a previous section, we talked about playing the "What if" game. This time, instead of playing *What if . . .* , why not play *I am . . . ?* How does one play? It all comes back to *being*. You can be what you want if you can picture yourself being it, living it, experiencing it. Close your eyes, relax, and imagine that you are successful. You live in a beautiful home. You have delicious relationships and vibrant health. You have a wonderful life. You are able to relax and enjoy life to the fullest. You are content, and all of your worries are gone. Use all five of your senses.

Now take it a step further and elaborate from there. In your Prosperity Journal, create your Dream Scene. Take a specific situation, circumstance, dream, or desire and literally write out the scene or the story about it in your Journal. Describe the way you want to see it unfold, and the way you want it to turn out. Remember, you are the star of your Dream Scene. Write as if you can see, taste, touch, smell, and feel your desired end result. Know that you are already there in your mind's eye. The key is that it must *feel good* while doing this process. The more detailed you can make it and feel good about it, the better.

Let's say you want a new home. What kind of house do you live in? Where is it located? Is this your summer home? What does the air smell like when you arrive at your home? Is it by the sea? Is it in the country? Can you see it clearly? How does it make you feel? Do you feel like it is really yours? Do you feel as though you've earned it, that you deserve all that you are visualizing? This, too, is part of the process. When your feelings are one with your thoughts and beliefs, and they are focused on the positive goals that you have set—the picture that you are holding in your mind's eye—they will begin manifesting. In essence, you are using your thoughts to attract the people, ideas, situations, and more that will bring you the vision you are holding of yourself. Thus, you create your reality.

Let go of limiting thoughts and begin by embracing the life that you want, desire, and deserve. Let the picture you see in your mind support your goals, and you will help them materialize that much faster. Let your dreams be the guide to your future and the road to your success. You just have to close your eyes and . . . *dream*.

YOUR FULL POTENTIAL

*The potential of the average person
is like a huge ocean unsailed, a new continent
unexplored, a world of possibilities
waiting to be released and channeled
toward some great good.*

Brian Tracy

Life Lesson #1
Live Life Fully

It's not so much what happens to us,
as what happens *in* us that counts.

Tim Hansel

Radical Sabbatical

I think all of us create our own miracles.

MICHAEL LANDON

It seems cliché, but here it is anyway: "When the student is ready, the teacher appears." The teacher, however, is not always a person. Sometimes the teacher appears simply as life, circumstances, or synchronicities. I call them road *signs*, those apparently random events that show up in my life that beg to be noticed. Like most people, I have an enormous capacity for brushing off *signs* as unimportant. What happens when I do? The *signs* turn into brick walls—those circumstances you crash into that stop you in your tracks.

In July 2001, my mother-in-law, Dorothy, gave me a great gift—a *sign*. She was diagnosed with probable ovarian cancer. Dorothy and I are very close and have an incredible mother/daughter relationship. She has been in my life since I was seventeen years old. My own mother died when I was twenty-three, and Dorothy has been a steady presence in my life.

Her diagnosis was the *sign* that finally gave me permission to stop what I was doing, something I had been talking about for months, but which seemed an impossible hurdle to jump. I had been promising to fire my current client, a contract that ate up all my time and energy, to embark on a sabbatical—something I had never experienced in thirty years of working. However, what I had not been able to give to myself, I gave to Dorothy. I was able to give her the gift of time by being there for her journey. A day after she and I were given this diagnosis, sitting side by side in her gynecologist's office, I gave my client notice.

An anxious few weeks followed as we waited for her referral to an oncology specialist in Ottawa, Canada. This was followed by more tests, family powwows, meetings with specialists, and finally surgery. Throughout the weeks that intervened, my husband, Jim, and I began to reach out to friends. For the first time in our lives, we called on others to form a prayer circle; everyone in our network was contacted. When the date and time of Dorothy's surgery was confirmed, this information was sent out. We were overwhelmed with everyone's generosity and their swift response to our request. What followed was, in my humble view, a miracle.

As Mom was wheeled into surgery, I planted myself in the waiting room. Jim and his youngest brother headed to the cafeteria to visit and grab a coffee. The waiting room was packed. Anxiety hung like a cloud over the heads of family members. I leaned my head back, resting it against the wall, closed my eyes, and imagined myself in the operating room with Dorothy. I could see her lying there as the surgeons and nurses moved with perfect precision around her. I counted myself down into my meditation place and called on Spirit. My intention was simple: "May Dorothy attract what is in her best interest and highest good."

As I followed my breath, I felt the energy around me and in me shift. A brilliant light filled my virtual meditation room. I could feel all the prayers that were being said for Dorothy at that moment, as if a thousand hands were holding mine as we formed a healing circle around her. I became a funnel channeling the energy from them to her. The light moved through me and embraced her as she lay there.

Finally, I spoke to her, "Mom, do you feel that? All the prayers people are sending you?"

"Yes," she said.

"Do you see how much you are loved?"

"I do," she answered.

"Do you really think you need this thing called cancer?"

"No, I don't think so."

With that response, she scooped her hands into her belly, held up two large tumors, and handed them to the surgeon.

"Here," she said, "I don't need these anymore."

I knew she had been healed. I stayed with her a few more minutes, holding that space of healing for her, and then returned to my physical surroundings and the quizzical looks of fellow waiting-room occupants. Seeing their faces, I wondered if I had also been healed, transformed by what had just occurred.

A few moments later, a voice from the reception desk called out, "A member of the Healey family, please."

I raced to the desk and took the phone as it was handed to me. "Yes?"

"To whom am I speaking?" the voice asked. "This is Betty Healey, Dorothy's daughter-in-law and the family spokesperson."

"I have excellent news, Mrs. Healey. Dorothy is going to be fine. We removed two grapefruit-size tumors, one from each ovary. They are what we call borderline tumors, non-cancerous but fast-growing. While we have to wait for the final pathology reports to confirm this, we feel sure that she will make a full recovery and require no further treatment."

"Thank you," I whispered.

Tears of gratitude streamed down my face. I turned away from the reception desk to a sea of anxious faces, all thinking I had received the dreadful cancer diagnosis. I couldn't speak, so I simply gave them all a thumbs-up sign and the best smile I could muster. Cheers filled the waiting room.

Dorothy did make a full recovery and just recently celebrated her seventy-eighth birthday. She walks to Mass every day, continues to keep active in various groups and charities, and looks after her children and grandchildren.

As for me, well, Dorothy didn't need me after she recovered, and I found myself on sabbatical. I took the next year off and dove into Julia Cameron's *The Artist's Way*. I began to write. I explored the depth of who I am and learned that I am important, just because I am, for "who I be" *not* "what I do." I also learned more about the power of prayer and intention, and how important it is in attracting the life I choose for myself. This has become my life's work.

How fortunate when Dorothy got sick that I could give to her what I had refused to offer to myself. How fortunate that she recovered, forcing me to look into that place inside myself and take the time to create space in my life for Spirit to enter.

Betty Healey, M.Ed.

Life Lesson #1: Live Life Fully

We're sure you've heard of the saying, "Live each day as though it were your last." Life is too short, and there are no guarantees. Why waste the chance to have all that you want? Live life to the fullest every step of the way. Just imagine the possibilities, then go out and make them your reality. Become the master of your destiny while you've the time to enjoy it and can mold it any way you want.

Exercise

Take a deep breath, close your eyes, and imagine how you'd respond to the following scenario:

You've been told that you have only two weeks left to live.

Now, after the shock wears off, what would you do next? How different would the next two weeks be compared to the way you've been living thus far? Would it be any different at all?

Take a look around at the day-to-day lives of your friends and family members. It seems to be human nature to put off one's idea of happiness until . . . "I graduate," "I earn and save more," "I get married," or "I'm done raising my family." *Then*, "I'll be able to play, to have fun and travel, or pursue my dream." What's up with that?

Why should all of the other things come first? Why not simultaneously? Have you wasted what could be very precious time by putting your life on hold until—whenever?

Somewhere along the line, society seems to have programmed us into believing that the majority cannot live life and be happy simultaneously. But there are many who throw caution to the wind and believe they can have the best of both worlds—and they do. They are living proof that it all comes down to *belief*.

If you believe that you can have the life you want, do the things you want with the people you want by your side, then the Universe will make it happen for you.

Would you have a long list of things to get done in those final two weeks, or would it be perhaps a more aggressive continuation of your day-to-day living?

Life Lesson #2
One Giant Leap for the Life You Love

A dream is not something that you wake up
from, but something that wakes you up.

Charlie Hedges

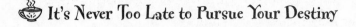

Never underestimate the power of
dreams and the influence of the human spirit.
We are all the same in this notion: the potential
for greatness lives within each of us.

WILMA RUDOLPH

As a professional speaker, I speak to thousands of people of all ages and from all walks of life each year. I constantly get feedback from those in their fifties, sixties, and seventies advising me that it is too late for them to create their own destiny. They believe they are too old, too broke, too out of shape, and too tired to do anything about their future. They stubbornly believe achieving prosperity is only for those in their twenties and thirties. Limited by their own personal beliefs, these people settle for less and never achieve prosperity.

The question I always ask my audience is the same question I pose to you: Are you creating your own destiny, or are you creating someone else's destiny? What do I mean by this? Consider the story of Cliff Young, a humble potato farmer in Australia, who consciously decided at age fifty-seven to create his own destiny. Up to this point his destiny was running the family farm and settling for a life of hard work. However, Cliff was quietly harboring a passion for long-distance running.

He came to the decision to live his own life and create his own destiny. Soon, he was seen in the wet Australian countryside training in a raincoat and gum boots. It did not matter to him that he was fifty-seven years of age and ill-equipped. After all his years on the farm, what mattered most to him was pursuing his passions. He ignored those who mocked him and the drivers who tried to run him off the back-country roads. He continued to train and built up to running twenty to forty miles per day.

In May 1983, after four years of constant training, Cliff Young shocked the world. At sixty-one years of age, he won the first Sydney-to-Melbourne ultramarathon—a distance of 875 kilometers (nearly 545 miles). To run this distance at any age is quite a feat, but to run it at sixty-one and beat some of the world's best-conditioned athletes in their twenties and thirties is absolutely incredible!

For years, running experts believed that the body needed a certain amount of sleep per night when running a grueling 100 miles per day. However, after falling far behind on the first day of the race, Cliff awoke at 1:00 AM and started running throughout the night. He surpassed the leaders, who slept to the usual 5:00 AM. Cliff's strategy worked so well that he continued to run each morning four hours earlier than his competitors. As a result of using this bold racing strategy, he astonished the world by crossing the finish line in first place. After five days, fifteen hours, and four minutes, Cliff Young emerged the victor!

News of Cliff Young's shocking victory traveled quickly throughout Australia. At his age, with his lack of experience and facing the world's best long-distance runners, no one thought he had a chance. He became a living legend, and the nation fell in love with this sixty-one-year-old potato farmer who saw the invisible and achieved the impossible. When talking about the prize money, Cliff was quoted as saying, "Ten thousand dollars—wow, that is a helluva lot of potatoes!" He then proceeded to share his prize money with the other competitors, acknowledging their preparation and hard work.

In 1984 and in 1987, at sixty-two and sixty-five, Cliff again competed in the ultramarathon. He continued using his 1:00 AM start-time routine. However, his strategy of waking at 1:00 AM instead of 5:00 AM soon became a widely accepted practice in this event. Cliff Young broke the paradigm, overcame self-doubt, and accomplished what no one thought remotely possible. Of greater significance is how he created his *own* destiny. He created a legacy of innovation and inspiration simply by following his passions, and was not limited by the beliefs held by so many others in their fifties, sixties, and seventies.

Patrick Snow

LIFE LESSON #2:
ONE GIANT LEAP FOR THE LIFE YOU LOVE

What's new in your life? Are you one of those exception-
ally perky people who make the average person cringe?
You know who I mean—the person with the permanent
smile, whether it's morning, noon, or midnight. This type of
person is high on life, just loves practically everything, and
puts a positive spin on anything that life dishes out. Are
you that person everyone loves to hate, but secretly
envies? Yes, they really do envy you because perky people
generally always have new experiences, new ideas, or new
adventures seemingly just waiting in the wings. Why?
Because their attraction principles are constantly operating in high gear.

If you're not a member of the perky club, here's a question
for you: When was the last new adventure that just seemed to
miraculously appear before you? What were you doing when
it occurred? Isn't it ironic that most people pray for miracles
when they are feeling their lowest, and then complain and
blame the Universe when their miracles don't come true?
Those pesky attraction principles just wreak havoc with people who don't pay attention to their inner workings.

Have you been finding that new opportunities are too few and far between for your liking lately? Perhaps if you take a current snapshot of a day in your life, you could find a way to turn things around so that abundance will become the norm.

Begin by looking at what's been holding you back. There are many things that seem to stand in the way of opportunity, but the primary culprit glares back at you whenever you look in the mirror. Fear is often a major player when it comes to naming obstacles on the path to your goals. Remember, fear is just a word unless you give it the power to become an action.

Are you ready to let go of the obstacles? Are you ready to take a leap and create a new reality for yourself? Although things rarely occur simultaneously, if you focus on one thing at a time, you can create an entirely new life for yourself piece-by-piece.

Exercise

1. Make a list of five things you would like to change, create, or experience. Once you have selected them, write a paragraph about the five things that will help bring them to life. Do this as if you'd actually achieved each one and are living life as you've created it. When you're finished with the descriptions, select the one that really makes your heart beat fastest. This will be your goal for the month, your single focus.

2. Map out how you will accomplish the goal. This is your first stepping stone toward creating the life you love, so be detailed while you assemble your action plan. Don't just say that you're going to lose ten pounds. Determine what specific steps you're going to take. For example, are you going to fast, diet, or exercise? If you're going to exercise, are you going to do it at a gym or at home, using equipment or a home video or DVD? These are the types of details that will focus you toward accomplishing your goal. The more detail provided, the less room for ambiguity.

Get onboard now. Take that one small step today for the giant leap toward the life that you will truly love—the one custom designed by *you*.

Life Lesson #3
If You Want It, You Can Have It

....

There is a difference between wishing
for a thing and being ready to receive it.
No one is ready for a thing
until they believe they can acquire it.
Before anything can come to us, we have to
envision it and believe that it is ours.

Napoleon Hill

☕ Transforming Thoughts

....

Your mind is a powerful magnet that will attract
to you the things you identify yourself with.

ALFREDO KARRAS

At 5:30 AM, the alarm went off faithfully as it did every morning. I woke up tired, depressed, and overwhelmed. It was time for me to start my day as the neighborhood babysitter. I felt much older than my twenty-two years. My husband at the time, thirteen years my senior, had five children with his former wife. Due to circumstances beyond their control, all five ended up living with us.

Even though my husband worked two jobs, I helped by babysitting and holding home parties. With two daughters under the age of three and five stepchildren ranging in ages from ten to fourteen, I sold everything from cosmetics to lingerie, but there never seemed to be enough to feed our family, pay our bills, and meet the mortgage.

It seemed as if we were plagued with one problem after another. One time the gas, electric, and water companies each pulled up in front of our house to collect or disconnect. I pleaded with them to give us one more day to scrape up enough to keep the services going. Thank God they did.

We didn't own much, and yet our home was burglarized

seven times! We had to decide whether to put bars on the windows or fix the leaky roof. We opted for the bars, and that winter it rained so hard that water poured through the ceiling. We placed a dozen pots throughout the house to catch the raindrops and used plastic to cover our beds.

Things went from bad to worse when my husband lost his second job. We were also about to lose our home and the car. I felt as if I had literally been pushed against the wall with no way out. Yet at the same time something within me screamed, "Some way, somehow, I am coming out of this!"

I decided to meet with a wise older friend, a very spiritual woman who understood universal principles. I told her about my situation, that my marriage was in trouble, and how I felt completely overwhelmed. I told her that I was worried all the time and frequently felt like I wanted to take my two children and run, but I just could not leave the others behind. "Everything in my life is going wrong," I said. "I'm not even twenty-five years old yet and I'm miserable!" With tears streaming down my face, I asked, "What is wrong? Why is God punishing me?"

She said, "Wanda, God is not punishing you, but if you think you're a victim, you become one. If you feel life is unfair to you, it only gets worse. If you want your life to get better, you have to see yourself beyond your circumstances. Thoughts that have brought you to this point cannot take you to where you want to go.

"Believe it or not, Wanda, your thoughts have creative power. What you think about and talk about influence how you feel. Your feelings influence what actions you'll take and what seems to show up in your life. Your actions impact your reality, and your reality then becomes your life. Making a positive change in your life must start with managing how you allow yourself to feel and what you allow yourself to listen to and speak about."

It did not come easy, but I was willing to try anything! We began to work together on processes that helped me control my emotional energy.

Not long after I had begun the practice of Energy Management, something extraordinary happened. I received a call from a man who had previously worked with my husband in the security department of a major department store. I hadn't spoken to him in years. He called just out of the blue and told me he was employed by a large corporation. He was in charge of awarding contracts to small businesses. He said that if my husband and I could get a private patrol license and do the other necessary paperwork, he thought he could be influential in getting us a very lucrative private patrol contract.

Well, we did all the necessary paperwork, got the license, submitted the proposal along with other companies, borrowed a desk and an old typewriter, moved the couch, and set up an office in the living room.

After a few weeks of waiting, we finally received a call—our bid had been rejected!

I was really disappointed, but not devastated because an unexpected transformation had taken place within me. I had come to believe that I could get my own contracts. I didn't need to be awarded anything. I began soliciting for business in my community the next day.

It was at this time that I really began to put into practice the principles I had been studying about the inherent connection we each have to a Higher Power. This awareness empowered me in a way that gave me the courage and confidence to do what I never believed previously possible.

There I was—a black woman of twenty-five with seven children in the home, a total of $500 (tax-refund check), my living room as an office, a telephone, a borrowed desk and a typewriter—trying to start a business in south-central Los Angeles. With creditors breathing down my neck, children being children, and living under the threat of being thrown out of our home and losing the car, I began the process of refusing to look at the circumstances that surrounded me. I chose instead to concentrate on the miracles trying to manifest before me.

I'll never forget those precious defining moments as I was driving up and down the streets looking for business. I would say an affirmation that my teacher reminded me to repeat, "Everywhere I go, I meet opportunity, I meet success, and I give thanks." This became not only my mantra, but my truth. As I knocked on doors, I felt this awesome tingle throughout my body. I felt myself actually smiling in anticipation of my first "Yes! Yes, we'll hire you!"

One morning, as I drove across town with no planned route, I ended up at a church on the east side of town. It was the middle of the week before noon and, only a couple of cars were in the parking lot. I noticed an open door up a long flight of stairs. The minister was in and willing to speak to me. Without any planned presentation or business card, I told him about our company—a company that didn't even have any guards yet. (I didn't tell him that part!)

Amazingly, after about twenty minutes, I walked out with a "Yes" and our first contract! Even though it was a mere thirteen hours of service a week, it seemed huge!

I felt an extraordinary sense of power, oneness, and a knowing that I had intentionally activated a process in which I was taking control of the steering wheel of my circumstances through this co-creative process with Spirit. What was so exciting was that I knew if it worked once, it would work again, and again, all the time. By the end of the first year, we were providing protection for more than thirty-five businesses and experiencing continued growth.

Three years later, our family was thrown into shock

when my husband had a stroke and died in his sleep. Meeting life on life's terms has been an important lesson for me. I've learned that no matter what happens in life, we are endowed with the power to connect with a Higher Source, which, when we listen, can guide us through the darkest times.

My company continued to expand and went from zero guards to 300. In the ten years I've been in business, well over 3,000 men and woman in our community have been provided employment.

The process of reconnecting daily with my inner guidance can make all things possible.

Wanda Peyton

LIFE LESSON #3:
IF YOU WANT IT, YOU CAN HAVE IT

In today's society, so much is based on scales, decided by tests, and judged by comparison. It's no wonder that society, as a whole, has issues about achievement and the quest for success. Success, like most other things, is viewed as a goal that has levels, and all too many people believe they are incapable of achieving true success. Why?

The dreams and desires of each person are just as important as the next, as is their fulfillment. But, when the Law of Attraction is so often overlooked, feelings of inferiority ensue. This especially occurs when you compare your dreams and accomplishments to those of others. So what happens when you think of Bill Gates or Donald Trump? Do you look at them and think, "I'll never see in a lifetime the kind of money that they see in a year?" Or do you smile and say, "Not yet, but I'm working on it." When you factor in the Law of Attraction, can you see how much more successful a person will be with an "I think I can" attitude versus an "I know I can't" attitude?

How can the Law of Attraction work for you? It will work when you focus on your perception of situations, accomplishments, and actions, and change them if you find yourself not measuring up to someone or something else. No one can force you into a role without a little help. You allow yourself to be forced into a role. This said, look at your perception of the kind of person who makes money, becomes a mega-star, or becomes the next Nobel Prize winner. Do any of these people look like you? If not, why not? Why should they be able to accomplish these things that are seemingly out of reach for you? In reality, they are not out of reach for you, but you have to draw that conclusion on your own and determine how to really make that perception shift. Once you have the answer to that question, the next step is to do something about it.

Would it be easier to reach your goal if you were better educated, dressed the part, or ran in the same circles as those who are where you'd like to be? Anything and everything is possible, and your job is to do what it takes to change your perception to make you believe it.

Exercise

Create reminders to reinforce the belief that nothing is keeping you from success. Write these reminders as inspirational quotes or daily affirmations that are strategically placed so that you can't help but see them often.

Your belief about what is possible is the core of the Law of Attraction, and more directly, the key to success and abundance. The only boundaries that can be placed on you are self-inflicted. Shed your limitations and get ready to embrace your destiny and vision—the vision that you hold for yourself, full of passion, promise, happiness, and success. If you want it, you *can* have it.

Life Lesson #4
You've Got It All

Think BIG! You are going to be
thinking anyway, so think BIG!

Donald Trump

 List for It

*The amazing thing about love is that
it is the best way to get to know ourselves.*

ROLLO MAY

I had taken our two small children and fled the house in fear for our safety more than once. After each event, John* would transform back into the charming man I'd fallen in love with, somehow convincing me that I was the cause of his outrageous behavior. He was always able to talk me back home. This made me question my own perception. *Was it me?* I didn't know when something I'd say or do might set him off.

Anxious and overwhelmed, I'd stay up late many nights, watching personal-development programs and searching for ways to make sense of our situation. Rocking and crying, over and over I'd lament, "How could this have happened to us?" I wondered if we could ever recover.

Completely distraught, I was barely able to get through the days. My best friend suggested a technique I hadn't used in years. "Make a list to define what you want," this wise woman said, "to see if John can be that."

I took out a fresh notebook. On top of the first page in capital letters I wrote: WHAT I WANT IN MY IDEAL

*Names have been changed.

LIFELONG COMPANION. I worked on that list for weeks, focusing on exactly what I wanted. I liked being married. I desperately wanted stability and a positive male role model for my children. What more did I want? Remarkably, my list grew to hundreds of very specific attributes, such as: irons better than I do, plays outside with the kids, sober, financially stable, brings out the best in me, self-assured.

In marked contrast to the desires of my younger self, the only physical attribute on the list was that he be "attractive to me." I looked at John, and then I looked at my list . . . could he be the one? I was still confused.

During this time, I attended a business conference. I flew from my home in Florida to Texas, and there I met thousands of people of widely diverse backgrounds from all over the country, all who believed in the transformational power of personal development. Milling around, making contacts in the lobby of the hotel and with no conscious thought of The List in mind, I was introduced to Steve.* He was described as "our token rocket scientist" from California.

As we sat in the midst of our colleagues, Steve and I chatted about the conference. Then, simultaneously, we stopped talking. We looked into each other's eyes. It was as if time stood still. It was not romantic, nor sexual; it was a profound connection. A hundred years of knowing in just one look. Someone asked a question, suddenly jarring us back to the physical reality of the hotel lobby. It was late. The group disbanded to get some sleep. In a few days, the conference came to a close.

Returning home, I was back in the despair I'd temporarily left behind. One day soon after, I caught sight of my six-foot-three, 220-pound husband chasing our small son into his bedroom. Running behind them, I arrived just in time to see him take his misplaced anger out on our son. I was dumbfounded. John had always made me feel responsible for his ugly outbursts. Surely, a six-year-old could not be held accountable. The refrain from a Brian Tracy telecast rang in my ears. "You become what you hang around most."

If I stay here, I will be just like him.

It was as if a switch was flipped. In that instant, I was clear about what I had to do.

The decision was hard, the follow-through still harder, but The List gave me courage. Certain a better life than this was waiting for me, I filed for divorce. Reviewing my list daily, I'd spend hours imagining what a solid partnership would be like with the man I'd envisioned.

My thoughts turned to Steve. He was thirty-seven, never married, no kids, a midwestern tractor mechanic turned west coast NASA engineer. I looked at my list and thought more about Steve.

Seems like a good candidate.

I picked up the phone and dialed his number.

"Hello, Steve? Yes, this is Hayley. We met at the conference in Dallas last summer. I'm getting divorced. How would you like to be the first in line?"

"No," he said. "First is a bad place to be." (Steve had been around the block a time or two.)

"How about first and last?" I asked.

"No, thanks," said Steve. Then he hung up.

Blatant rejection did not deter me. I picked up a pen and wrote, "I feel as if I know you, but I don't really know you. What I do know, I like very much. I want to know what kind of car you drive, what political thoughts you have, your dreams and aspirations, what confidences you haven't told a soul, and whether I will be privileged enough to ever share them someday. I really want to know you. Do you want to let me?" I popped it in the mail.

A few days later, I called again. This time, Steve did not hang up. We began the process of getting to know each other over the phone. We talked several nights a week.

At one point he said, "I feel as if I'm being interviewed. Have you got a list or something?"

"Yes, as a matter of fact, I have," I said.

"Why do you have a list?" he asked.

And so I told him about my list. "When I get what I want, it's because I have been very specific. I have been taught, *What you want wants you.* When what I want involves others, I first explore what I want. Then, independent of my outcome, I explore what they want in as great detail and from as many angles as possible. When our independently designed outcomes match, then it's time to research if they have in the past produced what they want at the same level, or greater, than I can produce what I want."

"I want to see that list!" he said.

"I'll show you mine when you show me yours," I replied.

Steve resolved to put the list he'd kept in his mind down on paper.

Next, we interviewed each other. Night after night, we shared our pasts and fantasized about our futures. We revealed our preferences, hobbies, habits, and plans. Miraculously, it seemed Steve possessed many of the attributes on my list! Months into courting this long-distance romance, it occurred to us that we ought to get together in person. Before making the trip, we exchanged our lists.

One balmy night six months later, we sat cuddling against a sand dune on Fort Lauderdale beach. Steve dug into his pocket, retrieving a very creased piece of paper. He opened it and handed it to me. On it was another list. It read:

> *Hayley Foster*
> *You are the love of my life*
> *I want to spend the rest of my life with you*
> *Will you marry me???*

Inscribed in our wedding bands is the Yiddish word *Bashert*—"meant to be."

Hayley Foster

LIFE LESSON #4:
YOU'VE GOT IT ALL

Amnesia is defined as partial or full memory loss. Many people are walking around right this moment forgetting who they really are. They have begun to believe what their environment is telling them. If you have been in a relationship that is abusive on any level, over a period of time you begin to tear away pieces of your soul. Every time you witness stress or listen to words that convey you just can't do anything right, you begin reprogramming your "worthiness software."

Many times the evidence we collect about ourselves is that we are simply not enough—not special, smart, motivated, clever, thin, organized, or focused enough. Nothing could be further from the truth, no matter who you are! You, your neighbor, your colleague, your children, your mate—all have everything it takes to experience the exact life each of you desires. The question is, "What do *you* desire?" You can't force others to shift their beliefs and actions, but you most certainly can change your own. Choose worthiness over "not enough," and you put yourself directly on the path of manifesting your every whim.

Your mind will collect an abundance of data to support whatever you are focused on. You are the chooser of what captures your attention, self-love or loathing. Have you ever listened to someone criticize themselves aloud? It's heart-wrenching. It's not attractive and makes others want to run for cover. Self-loathing, to any degree, is at the bottom of the vibrational scale.

It is really quite easy to find things to appreciate about yourself. Just look. Yes, your mother may have told you not to be conceited or that it's not appropriate to toot your own horn, but this may be the one thing she was misguided about. Feeling good about who you are and where you're going has nothing to do with being an egomaniac. In regard to the Law of Attraction, believing you can attract your desires means you accept that you are worthy. How can you believe good things are coming your way if you don't think you deserve it? You deserve because you were born. There are no hoops to jump through or a deserving person's checklist to fill out before you can have your desires met.

Living your full potential is about drawing out all that you are. Experience yourself fully by connecting to all that is perfect about you. There is no need to search for focus, skill, beauty, or any other talent. You already have it inside you. When you reach for it, it will be there. Practice and attention to these things will amplify them. The more you tap into them, the more they will radiate out into the world like magnets attracting every little and big desire that crosses your mind. Perfection is not about avoiding mistakes and doing things perfectly. It's about embracing the perfection of all that is.

When you are able to embrace the joyful moments, the contrasting experiences, awkward encounters, and creative bursts, resistance to life drops gently to the floor. This will create the space you need to thrive versus drive you into frustration and despair. You can always desire to be more masterful at what you practice without making yourself wrong about where you currently stand.

Exercise

Who are you really? What qualities make up the real *you*? In your Prosperity Journal, take a moment to do a self-inventory. Ask a few people who know you well to list five to ten words that describe you. This will help you get a clear picture. Do your best not to judge any qualities. If there are some that you can't quite bear to embrace, ask yourself how this quality may serve you. What if being quirky turned out to be what people found most endearing about you?

Reprinted by permission of Off the Mark and Mark Parisi. ©1993 Mark Parisi.

Life Lesson #5
Your Wealth Depends on You

It's kind of fun to do the impossible.

Walt Disney

Shake That Money Tree

> *Money never starts an idea; it's the*
> *idea that starts the money.*
>
> MARK VICTOR HANSEN

I found abundance on the back of a Harley. While my boyfriend Bruce gave me the thumbs-up sign, I gripped the silver bars attached to my seat, praying I wouldn't fling out sideways and down the sheer drop-offs on either side of this winding road. Roaring up a mountain had seemed like a good idea. After all, it would lift us up and away from the 100-degree deserts of Tucson, Arizona. But the heights dizzied me. And this was only my second ride. I sent out an urgent request to whatever Patron Saint of Motorcyclists might be on duty. "Right now! Get us safely up this mountain. And back down again."

My panic was elevated by my current state of financial alarm. I'd recently moved into my own little home after building up a fruitful career of editing, ghostwriting, and coaching. Almost instantly, three of my steady-paying clients suffered sudden personal or financial crises and vanished.

I felt like the guy in the *Austin Powers* movie who freezes and screams "Ahhhhhhhhhhh!" as he spots a ridiculously slow-moving steamroller in the far distance heading straight toward him. Instead of running or even tiptoeing out of the way, he keeps his eyes glued to the barely moving steamroller until it eventually flattens him.

Although I knew fluidity in thought was key to creating any satisfying change, I couldn't shake the images of my doomed financial future rolling toward me. My monthly payments now felt like a guillotine hanging over my head versus a thank-you for the joy of living in my own home. *What do I do? Now? Today? What do I do to bring in money instantly while having the time and energy to honor the projects I am already working on?*

Why not ride a Harley? It seemed as good a solution as any, even with the runaway fear. Ecstatic about his new bike, Bruce had been longing to share the adventure with me. Little did he realize that he'd be sharing this trip with all the Etheric Motorcycle Guides I could summon, too. I imagined them straddling the Harley with us, surrounding the bike with love and ease, keeping us free from falling rocks and fast cars. Soon, I sent these Saints of Safety to all the people on the mountain, and then to all the people who ever had or ever would travel on this road.

My grip relaxed. I peeked around at the voluptuous sweep of saguaros, ocotillo, and other nameless greenery. Before I knew it, I caught the scent of pine trees and felt the whispers of cool air. The mountain sang my heart back to me. Memories of other supreme moments of joy and expansion enfolded me. I began radiating blessings out to my family and friends, feeling like a reveler in a parade tossing out beads and balloons.

When we arrived safely back to Bruce's house, I was filled with such bliss that I started journaling out my gratitude. This was abundance, this richness of heart. Now how could I extend this energy to my finances?

Then an answer struck. If we each possess an innate inner wisdom, there must be a living part of me that knew exactly what I needed in that moment to create immediate financial abundance in my life. Not the someday kind of abundance I'd always put on a pedestal. Not the kind that happens only if I'm in a good mood forever and chant, "I am worthy" every day for ten years while breathing through my left nostril. From this place of deep appreciation, I imagined myself connecting to my Inner Abundance Team. I playfully wrote out a request for immediate abundance— now, today.

Two minutes later, the phone rang. It was my boyfriend's dad saying he'd like to pay our way for a three-week cruise to Hawaii, a trip I'd let go of months ago because I didn't have the money. What fun! I laughed and waved my journal in my boyfriend's face.

In the past, I would have taken Hawaii as the response to my abundance request and gone my merry way. This time I recognized it as a grand "ta-da!" to catch my attention. It was a dramatic reminder that if reality was truly fluid, and fear only made it appear frozen, then I had plenty of space and time to shape any outcome. Nothing was inevitable.

I didn't have to keep waking up at 3:00 AM, recreating the image of my financial future as a steamroller about to flatten me. I had lots of wiggle room. Feelings of appreciation and wonder inspired that wiggle room, that sense of spaciousness and possibility. All I had to do was slow down my thoughts enough to examine them with fine tweezers. What thoughts sparked feelings of delight? What thoughts crushed me?

Not too long ago, I would have tried to crush the thoughts that seemed to crush me. Now I invited all my thoughts and the feelings they inspired into the same room. When I felt disappointment, I didn't swat it away, hold my breath, or deny it was there. I allowed it. What a relief! The relief led to acceptance. Acceptance led to a better thought. And, as Abraham-Hicks teaches through Esther and Jerry Hicks, reaching for a better thought creates miracles.

What I wanted was a gentle revolution—daily, consistent prosperity in a practical, cash-in-hand kind of way. And that's what I got. Within a week, I had two new clients. In two more weeks, a co-author handed me an envelope filled with unexpected royalties. Then a woman I respected hired me to collaborate with her on a book about healing with sound. *Ahhhhh* is a sound that opens the heart.

From *Ahhhhh!!!* to *Ahhhhhh* . . . in sixty thoughts or less. On or off the Harley, that's one journey I gladly take.

Jan Henrikson

LIFE LESSON #5:
YOUR WEALTH DEPENDS ON YOU

What if it were truly easy to deliberately take a thought and be responsible for aligning yourself with that thought? What if you decided that every feeling, experience, and material item you desired was easily accessible to you? What if it were as easy to manifest $1,000,000 as a penny? What if the key to all this was being curious enough to test these theories? It's all a decision away if you so choose to take on the adventure.

The adventure begins with accepting that it's not just the Rockefellers, Ted Turners, and Donald Trumps of the world who can be wealthy. You can embrace the same mindset as they've had and watch your wealth increase to new heights. What was their process to create wealth?

They had a vision, which was exciting enough to move them into desire. This desire became the channel for their inspired ideas and actions.

This is no different from the basic steps of the Laws of Attraction. It's always the same process internally, but everyone's path looks different from the outside. It works to lock onto the idea of the vision or what the wealth will give you. There are no right or wrong ways to get there, as long as there is fire behind the desire that lights you up. If your heart is singing, that's your inner being saying, "Yes!"

When your desire is backed by the feeling of it's never enough, you'll always feel like not enough. A desire backed by pure positive thoughts is the only formula you need.

As with all desires, financial prosperity is not about choosing the exact actions that you've read in an investing book. Once you align your focus with the desire, the perfect choices for you will be easy for you to land on. If you were focusing your attention on bankruptcy and decided to make some new investments, what do you think your results might be? You could walk in the footsteps of Warren Buffett, but if you weren't believing that wealth was possible for you, you'd have a painful trip to the bank.

If you're one of those people who has been focused on struggle or feeling like you're not enough, opening yourself up to receiving can feel awkward. Accepting your worth may take some practice. If somebody offers you assistance and it would make your life easier, would you accept it? Every time? Would you consider it cheating if you allowed your desires to manifest without struggle? What if you accepted that ease and flow to all of your desires were part of the recipe that the Universe created? Ask and it will be given. Your magic lamp is in the house. Please dust it off and begin using it immediately.

Exercise

Today, allow things to unfold easily. If you catch yourself pushing a task through or trying to talk someone into giving you your way, stop. If you find yourself worrying about something turning out the way you want, stop. Breathe.

Allow the Universe to assist you. If a friend or colleague can take the load off of you, ask. If you were the queen or king of the kingdom, how would you handle it? How easy are you willing to let it be? Practice ease today.

Beware: allowing yourself to receive may be addicting. We highly promote it.

ACTS OF FAITH

Faith is putting all your eggs
in God's basket, then counting
your blessings before they hatch.

Ramona C. Carroll

Reprinted by permission of Off the Mark and Mark Parisi. ©2006 Mark Parisi.

Life Lesson #1
The Secret to Making It B-I-G

You see things, and you say, "Why?"
But I dream things that never were,
and I say, "Why not?"

George Bernard Shaw

What Is the Best Use of a Life Given This Much Good Fortune?

....

I have no doubt whatever that most people live,
whether physically, intellectually, or morally, in a
very restricted circle of their potential being . . .
we all have reservoirs of life to draw upon of
which we do not dream.

WILLIAM JAMES

In 1987, Lynne, a woman I hardly knew, asked me to give $5,000 to an organization committed to end hunger on the planet. I didn't have $5,000. I had a company, a mortgage, and a couple thousand dollars in savings. I told her that I was committed to the end of global hunger, but that I didn't have the money. Her next words changed my life, and I will never forget them. "Well, go make it." It sounded like a wild idea, so I did it. And then I gave her the money.

The next year, Lynne called again and asked me for $20,000 for the same organization. I explained that the $5,000 I gave was far more money than I had ever given to any organization, and although I supported her vision, I just didn't have $20,000. I could have seen it coming. She again suggested that I go make it and that I would then truly become a philanthropist. I did. I went out and made it, and I became a philanthropist.

The next year, she asked for $100,000. By then I had made it, and I said, "Yes." I believe that one of the biggest contributing factors to my wealth was this choice to become a philanthropist. I believe that money flows most easily to people who have clear, compelling, and compassionate uses for it.

Since hearing Lynne's words, I have contributed several million dollars to philanthropic projects. I have actually contributed almost as much money as I have kept. Some may call this foolish. I'm here to suggest otherwise.

Giving away money was the best thing I had ever done, and it continues to be one of the best things I do. In many ways, it is a selfish act. It gives me more pleasure than if I used that money to buy something for myself or my family.

I made this money by starting a publishing and consulting company in 1981. I took out a $10,000 second mortgage on my house and started working part-time at my new company while continuing to work full-time at the college where I had been teaching for six years. Not wanting to risk too much, I continued working at the college for the next two years while developing the business. I didn't leave the security of working for another until I had six full-time employees.

This publishing and consulting company got off to a slow start, but soon began to flourish, mostly because we didn't know what we were doing, and we didn't ask traditional publishers how they did it. Instead, we invented what we thought would work best without regard to what others had already done. Because we didn't know how it was "supposed to be done," we created a publishing company that outperformed all others. Our little publishing company in the Black Hills of South Dakota created "Becoming a Master Student," which became the best-selling college text in America for over a decade. We outsold all the major publishing companies from New York, Boston, and Chicago.

We were also successful because we created long-range goals and then created the mid-range and short-range goals by imagining ourselves in the future and planning backwards, by describing how we imagined we got to achieve that successful future. One of these long-range goals was to "pay the rent by noon." What it meant was that I wanted to be able to get to a point where I only worked half-days to make a living and then spent the other half-day making a difference. The company became a reflection of my commitment to contribute significantly to improve the quality of life for the poorest of the poor.

Another reason we were so financially successful is that we created a list of values that we would operate from. One of our most important values was *fun*. I knew that if we were going to take on big projects, it would be hard to sustain the effort and attract others to them unless it was fun.

In addition to creating long-range goals and a clear set of values, we also created a 100-year plan that clearly outlined all the goals that we wanted to be fulfilled even after we died. This all might seem impractical, but the result was unpredictable financial success. By 1989, I had "paid the rent by noon." At that time, I was able to spend more of my day making a difference in the world than I did making a living. I loved it. So, I set another goal to be able to pay the rent by 8:00 AM.

Essentially, I wanted to retire from the job of making a living and use my days contributing in the most effective way I knew to improve the quality of life for the 1.3 billion people on our planet who live on less than a dollar a day. These people live in abject poverty. They have little to eat, no clean drinking water, housing that we wouldn't even subject our animals to, and little or no hope.

By 1993, I got to the place where I could retire from making a living and move fully into making a difference. Since then, I have worked full-time for no pay.

With this freedom to contribute, I keep looking for the best way that my staff and I can contribute our time and money. Many times a week I ask myself, "What is the best use of a life given this much good fortune?"

This wonderful life of contribution all started when

Lynne simply would not accept my perfectly legitimate excuse for not giving her $5,000. When she countered my "No" with "Go out and make it," she helped me transcend my limited thinking so I could go on to create a wonderful life rich with contribution.

Dave Ellis

LIFE LESSON #1:
THE SECRET TO MAKING IT B-I-G

Do you dream big? Do you use all of your faculties to imagine that you can obtain your wildest, biggest, seemingly impossible dream? Now that you've imagined it, have you asked yourself how to get it? If not, that could be what suspends your forward progress.

The mind is a wonderful thing. It works day and night to solve the things that are presented to it. In fact, it won't stop until we acknowledge that the result is to our liking. How often have you pushed something out of your consciousness, only to have it resurface in your dreams? That's the mind still working on the solution that you requested.

The problem most of the population faces is that they dream too small. How often have you found yourself asking for a new job, a raise, or a couple of new clients? While you may have effectively mastered asking and manifesting your requests, you could be asking, "How do I earn or create a million dollars?" In other words, think, dream, and question big! Imagine putting the mind to work on that one!

There is a story about a young man named Joel who sat by the water staring ahead, but he was not seeing the glorious view or appreciating the beautiful day. Instead, he was buried in distress. He had just a few days to come up with the money to make his bills, and he was horribly short. So he sat by the water trying to think of ways to secure the much-needed cash. Borrowing the money was out. Overtime would provide the funds, but not in time. While he was contemplating his dilemma, an older gentleman of about seventy sat down at the other end of the bench. After a few moments, he asked Joel why he had such a heavy heart. Joel replied that his finances were strained month after month, and this month was the worse yet.

The older gentleman looked at Joel for several seconds and replied, "So, what are you going to do about it?" To this, Joel snapped, "Well, if I knew that, I wouldn't be sitting here!" The older gentleman thought for a moment and said, "I think that you have finally found the problem." To this, Joel looked at him with exasperation clearly etched on his face.

The older gentleman drew a deep breath and began to explain it slowly. "You see, young fellow, you have spent so much time dwelling on how to meet your monthly obligations that you have not spent any time trying to solve your lifetime obligations. I don't mean the financial obligations to others, but the ones you owe to yourself. So, I suggest that you broaden your line of sight and try to determine how you're going to make your success for one year, ten years, twenty years, and finally a lifetime. Don't fret. Ask the questions, and the answers will come. In the meanwhile, you'll find your daily, weekly, and monthly expenses will take care of themselves."

The older gentleman got up from the bench, tipped his hat to Joel, and carefully made his way back down the path. At the end of the path, Joel saw a chauffeur waiting patiently for the gentleman, with the door held wide. Joel looked after him for a few minutes and decided then and there to put the advice given to him to use. He figured that he had nothing to lose, and the old gentleman must know a bit about what he suggested if he could afford a chauffeur-driven limousine.

Are you going to take the advice of the old gentleman, too, and broaden your line of sight? Are you asking the big questions and letting the little ones fall into place on their own?

Exercise

Tuning in to the big questions and broadening your line of sight can be done in a number of ways—through guided meditation or relaxation techniques, yoga, a long bubble bath, or a turn in the steam room—as long as it helps you relax and can get you tuned into what you are feeling.

It helps immensely to record your dreams and feelings in your Prosperity Journal, especially when you are working on the big questions that require multiple writing sessions. In addition, your Journal allows you to keep track of the things you want to accomplish and lets you glimpse your thoughts in that exact moment, so that you can see how everything unfolds. Your Journal is your way of recording life scene by scene. It helps to write things out when you need to see how they fit together, and make sure that what you thought at 3:00 AM was really as good as what you thought at 9:00 AM. The plus side is that you are sure to remember what you were thinking.

Let your mind do what it does best in answering the questions and solving the problems for you. Just remember that you asked the question. So be on the lookout for the answer when it comes. Please note the usage: *When* it comes, not if. The answer *will* come.

Life Lesson #2
Givers Always Gain

Think of giving not as a duty,
but as a privilege.

John D. Rockefeller, Jr.

No one has ever become poor by giving.

Anne Frank

Here's something I discovered a few decades ago:

If you want money, you only have to do one thing.

It's the one thing some of the wealthiest people on the planet have done and are doing.

It's the one thing written about in various ancient cultures and still promoted today.

It's the one thing that will bring money to anyone who does it, but at the same time most people will fear doing it.

What is that one thing?

John D. Rockefeller did it since childhood. He became a billionaire.

Andrew Carnegie did it, too. He became a tycoon.

What is the greatest money-making secret in history? What is the one thing that works for everyone?

Give money away.

Give it to people who help you stay in touch with your inner world.

Give it to people who inspire you, serve you, heal you, and love you.

Give it to people without expecting them to return it, but

give it knowing it will come back to you multiplied from some source.

In 1924, John D. Rockefeller wrote to his son and explained his practice of giving away money. He wrote, ". . . in the beginning of getting money, way back in my childhood, I began giving it away, and continued increasing the gifts as the income increased . . ."

Did you notice what he said?

He gave away more money as he received more income. He gave away $550 million in his lifetime.

Some people think Rockefeller started giving away dimes as a publicity stunt to improve his image. That's not true. The public-relations man who worked for Rockefeller was Ivy Lee. In *Courtier to the Crowd*, a great biography of Lee, Ray Eldon Hiebert states that Rockefeller had been giving money away for decades on his own. All Lee did was let the public know.

P. T. Barnum gave money away, too. As I wrote in my book about him, *There's a Customer Born Every Minute*, Barnum believed in what he called a "profitable philanthropy." He knew giving would lead to receiving. He, too, became one of the world's richest men.

Andrew Carnegie gave enormously, too. Of course, he became one of the richest men in America's history.

Bruce Barton, cofounder of the famous BBDO advertising agency and the key subject of my book *The Seven Lost*

Secrets of Success, also believed in giving. In 1927 he wrote: "If a man practices doing things for other people until it becomes so much a habit that he is unconscious of it, all the good forces of the Universe line up behind him and whatever he undertakes to do." Barton became a best-selling author, business celebrity, contributor to numerous causes, and very wealthy.

While some might argue that these early tycoons had the money to give, so it was easy for them, I would argue that they got the money in part because they were willing to freely give. The giving led to the receiving. The giving led to more wealth.

I'll repeat that:

The giving led to the receiving.

The giving led to more wealth.

Today it's fashionable for businesses to give money to worthy causes. It makes them look good, and of course it helps those who receive it. Anita Roddick's Body Shop stores, Ben Cohen and Jerry Greenfield's ice cream, and Yvon Chouinard's Patagonia are living examples of how giving can be good for business.

But what I'm talking about here is individual giving. I'm talking about you giving money so you will receive more money.

If there's one thing I think people do wrong when they practice giving, is that they give too little. They hold on to their money and let it trickle out when it comes to giving.

And that's why they aren't receiving.

You have to give, and give a lot, to be in the flow of life to receive.

I remember when I first heard about the idea of giving. I thought it was a scheme to get me to give money to the people who were telling me to do the giving.

If I did give, it was like a miser. Naturally, what I got in return was equivalent to what I gave. I gave little. I got little.

But then one day I decided to test the theory of giving.

I love inspiring stories. I read them, listen to them, share them, and tell them. I decided to thank Mike Dooley of www.tut.com for the inspiring messages he shares with me and others every day by e-mail.

I decided to give him some money. In the past, I would have given him maybe five dollars. But that's when I came from scarcity and feared the giving principle wouldn't work. This time would be different. I took out my checkbook and wrote a check for one thousand dollars.

One thousand dollars!

At that time, it was the largest single contribution I had ever made in my life.

Yes, it made me nervous. But it mostly made me excited. I wanted to make a difference. I wanted to reward Mike. And I wanted to see what would happen.

Mike was stunned. He got my check in the mail and nearly drove off the road as he headed home. He couldn't believe it. He even called to thank me. I enjoyed his boyish surprise. It made me feel like a million bucks. (Note that!)

I loved making him so happy. I delighted in giving the money to him. Whatever he did with it was fine with me. I received an incredible feeling of helping someone continue doing what I believed in. It was an inner rush to help him. I still rejoice at sending him the money.

And then something wonderful began to happen.

I got a call from a person who wanted me to co-author his book, a job that ended up paying me many times over what I had given away.

And then a publisher in Japan contacted me, wanting to buy the translation rights to my best-selling book, *The Attractor Factor.* They, too, offered me many times what I had given Mike as a gift.

A true skeptic can say these events are unrelated. Maybe in the skeptic's mind, they aren't. In mine, they are.

When I gave money to Mike, I sent a message to myself and to the world that I was prosperous and in the flow. I also set up a magnetic principle that attracted money to me: As you give, so you will get.

Give time, and you'll get time.

Give products, and you'll get products.

Give love, and you'll get love.

Give money, and you'll get money.

This one tip alone can transform your finances. Think of the person or persons who have inspired you over the past week. Who made you feel good about yourself, your life, your dreams, or your goals?

Give that person some money. Give them something from your heart. Don't be stingy. Come from abundance, not scarcity. Give without expecting return from that person, but do expect return. As you do, you will see your own prosperity grow.

That is the Greatest Money-Making Secret in History!

Joe Vitale

LIFE LESSON #2:
GIVERS ALWAYS GAIN

Do you know the quickest way to build your financial empire? It's not by saving, investing, or getting a second job. Nor is it by anything dishonest or unethical. It's by giving and sharing. That's right, giving money to causes and organizations that you value personally is the fastest way for prosperity to grow.

You may be wondering, "How can this be? If I give my money away, I'll have less of it!" Well, the answer is . . . yes and no. Yes, you will initially be using the funds that you have, but no because you will gain more than you gave away. How? Prosperity occurs because the Universe takes care of you for your selfless generosity. Some of the wealthiest people in the world, both past and present, created more wealth for themselves by contributing to others. Look at Oprah. How much money has her Angel Network given away to date? For years, Oprah has contributed a portion of her income, often anonymously, yet her wealth continues to grow, and her life seems abundant.

How can you adopt a giving lifestyle? It's easy to do. Just make a commitment to give from your heart . . . be it money, time, information, or love. It allows you to help make a difference in and to the things that matter most to you. You get to witness firsthand the good that your contribution can do, and you typically get paid back exponentially. What a bonus!

Can you imagine the long-term effects of the prosperity that would explode in this country if everyone embraced this concept? Benefits would flow to the masses—children's groups, organizations, medical research, neighbors in need, and elderly care, among so many other worthy causes. Consider also the personal benefits you could reap—available funds to pay off debt, to start a new business, to retire with ease, and the ability to enjoy life without monetary stress.

A church began embracing this idea several years ago and has raised its community up from poverty, one family and one debt at a time. The movement began when the head of the church found out there was a family home facing repossession within days. He wanted to help them, but there was no extra money in the church coffers. So during his next sermon, he asked his parishioners to help them out and sent around the collection plate. They collected enough money for the family to become current on their payments, with a little extra to help them get on their feet. He then decided to do this routinely as a means to help his parishioners dig out from under the heavy load of debt they were carrying. As a community, they work together to help each other through selflessness. They can rest assured that the Universe will give back to them the generosity they so willingly bestowed upon their neighbors.

So take a lesson from this community and let giving pave the way for you to create all that you desire. Selflessness can indeed make you rich . . . in heartfelt joy and of deep pockets. Make a commitment, and you can reap what you sow.

Exercise

Identify a person, cause, or organization that is close to your heart and make a commitment to contribute to them.

Once you start, write down in your Prosperity Journal the new financial opportunities that begin showing up. Some of the things that others have manifested are new job offers for a larger salary, new clients, new business ideas, partnerships or contacts resulting in more funds, unexpected payments, and so forth.

It's your gift, and you have control over deciding where it would provide the greatest benefit. This alone should make you feel good inside. Being able to help those less fortunate is always powerful with the Universe. It shows that you are grateful for what you have and willing to help those who provide value to you and others. Think of how beneficial your gift will be. Those on the receiving end will give thanks for the gift that you gave and put their gratitude out into the Universe as well. The more you give, the greater the number of people who benefit in a positive prosperous way. This creates more opportunity for you to give by making more available to you.

Life Lesson #3
Your Intuition Knows

> Faith is believing in things
> when common sense tells you not to.
>
> *George Seaton*

☕ The Valentine's Day Cruise

A good friend of mine, who owns a travel agency, introduced me to the delightful experience of traveling by cruise ship. In addition, I got to travel with her at a special rate, so it felt even more magical. For me, there is something special on a cruise. An experience of relaxation I don't feel anywhere else. Perhaps it is the beautiful surroundings, the extra attention given to personal service, the sumptuous food, or the atmosphere where everyone is relaxing and enjoying themselves. Or perhaps it is because I am separated from all of the things in my daily life that keep me busy, and the biggest decision or task of the day is deciding what to eat and what activities most appeal to me.

A few years ago, one of the ships we had traveled on was in port in Honolulu. We got a pass to go onboard while they were preparing for a new group of passengers. As I walked around this beautiful ship, seeing my reflection in the mirrors and polished brass, remembering the laughter and the childlike way I anticipated each new day on board, I remembered the fun times I had on my last cruise. I felt this deep, strong desire to be cruising again. I mentioned this desire to my friend, and she was *not* encouraging, saying it was a busy time and not likely to happen.

I wasn't willing to let go of the thought that easily (a good

Law of Attraction clue!) and asked one of the crewmembers when the ship would be back in Honolulu. He said it would be back in two weeks, sailing from Hawaii to Ensenada, Mexico. I got really excited and said to my friend, "Judy, we have to be on this ship in two weeks!" She explained that wasn't possible for a number of reasons—her mother was coming to visit from out of state during that time, and besides, the ship was fully booked.

I said, "I don't know how, but I *know* we will be on this ship sailing for Mexico in two weeks. Will you do me a favor and at least call the office and see if we can be put on a waiting list?" She said she would call, but it would do no good. Besides, she couldn't be gone when her mother was visiting. A crewmember confirmed that the ship was sold out. I ignored it all and simply stayed connected to the strong desire to be back on the ship. I drove my friend crazy, chattering about how great it would feel to be back on a cruise, and how I didn't care if she believed me or not; I just knew we were going to do it!

The next day, Judy called to tell me that she had checked with the cruise line, and not only was the ship sold out, but there were twelve full-fare couples on the wait list! Even if there were some last-minute cancellations, it was not possible that twelve cabins would cancel in less than two weeks. I repeated to Judy, "I don't know how, but I know we will be on the next sailing of the ship, and please just humor me and put us on the wait list."

She said she still couldn't go, but to humor me, she would do it, since there was no chance of getting on anyhow. Every time I spoke with Judy over the next few days, I kept telling her she had better get packed as we were sailing on the fourteenth!

A few days later, Judy called and said that I must have been sending out some strong vibes since she got a call from her mother saying the visit would be postponed for a week. Her mother wanted to arrive the day after the cruise ended! But after her mother's call, Judy checked with the cruise line, and we were still number thirteen on the wait list. The cruise was barely a week away.

Three days before the cruise was to begin, I called Judy and told her to start packing. Judy reminded me that we still didn't have a cabin, and I said, "I don't know how, but I know we will be on that ship in three days!"

The day before the ship was due to sail, Judy called me, sounding quite shocked. She said she had just received a call from the cruise line, and they asked if she was still interested in a cabin. If so, she could have one, and at her discounted rate. She asked what had happened to all of the other passengers on the wait list. She was told there was just one last-minute cancellation, but all the full-fare passengers on the wait list lived in other states, and it was too late for them to get to Honolulu.

On February fourteenth, as I had known all along, we boarded the ship. I was grinning from ear to ear in my delight to be on the cruise, and I was elated to experience what I came to know as the Law of Attraction.

Maureen O'Shaughnessy

LIFE LESSON #3:
YOUR INTUITION KNOWS

Your intuition is your guide, the one thing you can truly count on that is always looking out for your best interest . . . if you choose to listen for it, not intercept the message, and act on its direction. It is the *knowing* you have about something without being able to explain it.

But it's very easy to let your voice of intuition get clouded by other things. Fear, desire, self-doubt, and over-reasoning are some of the many types of intuition blockers. Trust that your intuition is your personal guide to the correct path for you at all times. Turn off whatever limiting beliefs may be overpowering your intuition.

Perhaps it's your belief that intuition is just "mumbo jumbo." It is easy to believe this because intuition is not thought of as a concrete thing. It is based on nonverbal things, feelings, unconscious thought, and instinct. This is definitely not a description for people who define things in black and white. Intuition is often looked at as gray. But it is not. Intuition is basically a synopsis of information that has been taken in through all of the senses, memory, subconscious, and reasoning. It is like a clear overview in Cliff Notes' format.

When your intuition speaks to you, do you hear it? Do you know how to identify it? Your intuition typically kicks in when you are quiet. Many people find answers to their questions in their dreams, or when meditating. Others find them "out of the blue," when they are not looking for them. Many *feel* the right thing to do or what the next course of action should be. There are many ways that your intuition will speak to you, and everyone's mode of recognition is unique.

Exercise

How does one learn to trust intuition? Like everything else, if it is practiced, it becomes second nature.

1. Sit in a quiet, comfortable place where you will not be disturbed. Allow yourself to consciously ask for the answers to something that you are seeking and write down the results when they occur in your Prosperity Journal. Visualize yourself unlocking a door and seeing your answer tumble from within.

2. Your plan to trust your intuition needs to be put into play. A well-thought-out plan is simply a well-thought-out plan unless it is put into motion. If you have a history of not trusting your instincts, why not start small? Try selecting what you *feel* is a good restaurant or a good book in order to build your confidence level. Follow it up with increasingly bigger events. Each success will bring you closer to following your instincts comfortably, and soon it will become second nature.

Remember, listening to yourself with full attention is the precursor to positive, successful attraction. You cannot attract what you want if you are not in command of the kinds of vibes you are shooting out into the Universe. So enjoy this process of becoming in tune with actions, thoughts, and feelings. The results will be well worth the effort when you let your intuition be your guide.

Life Lesson #4
Putting Actions to Your Intentions

Since it doesn't cost a dime to dream,
you'll never shortchange yourself
when you stretch your imagination.

Robert Schuller

If you have a dream, give it a chance to happen.

RICHARD DeVos

For years, I had wanted to be able to live within walking distance of the ocean, preferably with a view.

"Well, views are at a premium, but I promise you'll have a view," my upbeat real-estate agent said.

And, sure enough, when I opened the bedroom window of my new home, stood on a little footstool, stuck my head all the way out the window, and peered down the alleyway through the rows of houses, I could see a lovely sliver of the Pacific. My dog and I thoroughly enjoyed our walks along the boardwalk, and when it rained and no one was out there to enforce the "no dogs allowed" sign, we went running all the way down the beach to the ocean.

And for a number of years, that was quite enough.

But then, that old bugaboo, "dreaming" came round once again. A house on the ocean with a real view became my new obsession. It was also ridiculously clear, as I drove up and down the coast of southern California, that I couldn't afford it.

"So what am I gonna do?" I asked my best friend.

"Create it. What else?" she exclaimed. "Do that thing

you're always talking about. Appreciate it into your existence."

"Well, that's fine for finding parking places or getting a raise," I replied, "but this? You know how expensive these homes are?"

She laughed. "You better put your money where your mouth is, Noelle. You're always saying the Universe doesn't care whether you're asking for dimes or dollars. Go for it!"

Sigh. Well, she was right. I couldn't very well teach how to appreciate wonderful things into your life if I couldn't do it myself. It's just that this was so big!

I sat up most of the night writing about my dream house. I set down on paper how joyous and free I would feel in my new home, how comfortable, safe, and secure it would be, a beautiful home filled with light, surrounded by trees, deep in nature, with a clear, open view of the ocean, and a big backyard for lots of pets. Then I set the paper aside and started dreaming.

Each day, for a little bit, I'd sit with my eyes closed and walk through my dream home. I'd invent it as I went along. Rooms would change as I imagined the house first one way, then the other. But, most importantly, I then would turn my attention to loving my condo and appreciating it as fully as I could, for I knew that only by appreciating what I already had would I attract what I now wanted. I repainted the bathroom, hung a piece of crushed forest-green velvet the whole length of one bedroom wall, and kept the place spotless. I said to anyone who would listen, "I love my place! I have such a great home."

I figured out what the mortgage would be on my dream home. After I picked myself up off the floor, I decided the only way I'd get over my utter panic at having to bring in that much income every month would be to practice actually doing it. So each month, in addition to my current mortgage, I deposited in a special savings account the additional amount I thought I'd need for my dream house mortgage. That sounds way easier than it was!

At first, I thought I'd be dining on macaroni for the rest of my days. Some months it seemed utterly impossible. But after a while, it got a little easier, and finally—two years down the pike—I found I didn't have to strain to set aside those additional dollars. I also found, much to my delight, the savings account I had refused to look at other than to deposit my monthly dollars had accumulated into a sizeable amount that I could use to help with the down payment. I decided I was ready.

I went to my wonderful, perpetually happy real-estate agent and said, "I'd like to find a place by the ocean with a *real* view."

"Oh, another condo?" she asked enthusiastically. "Sure."

"No," I gulped. "This time I'd like to buy a house." Silence.

Very gently, she asked, "Are you sure, dear?"

I took a deep breath and said, "Yes-I'm-sure-but-we-have-to-sell-the-condo-at-the-same-time-or-I-won't-be-able-to-do-it," all in one breath, which my sweet real-estate agent somehow understood. She beamed, we shook hands, and that was that.

Two weeks later on my way to a speaking engagement, I passed my real-estate agent hammering a "Sold" sign into place. "Oh, Noelle, I'm so glad I caught you," she said. "I have a buyer for your condo."

"But I haven't even begun looking for my new home!" I sputtered.

"Oh, that's all right. We'll find it," she waved as I drove off.

It left me wondering, *Now what am I going to do?*

The next day, my real-estate agent showed me "a lovely little place, dear, perfect for a single gal," which was indeed lovely. It was, however, squished between two very large McMansions, and the view of the ocean, although better than the view I presently had, still required numerous physical gyrations. I declined. A couple of days later, my real-estate agent chit-chatted merrily for what seemed like hours as we drove way into the back portions of Malibu to finally come upon a house, all by itself, a cement block set in desolate scrub.

"Very modern," my real-estate agent said. "Just the thing

for a professional such as yourself." I pointed out that the view of the ocean was so distant that I could barely tell it was ocean. "Well, given what you can afford," my real-estate agent confided, "this is about as good as you'll get."

I knew she was right, but I couldn't just settle for less than my dream. "I love my condo," I told her. "It's not worth moving if I can't have my dream home." I went home, despondent, wondering if I'd been wrong all along. Maybe I couldn't appreciate my dream into existence. Maybe I'd just been fooling myself. I had a restless night, and woke up grouchy and depressed.

My girlfriend called: "Did you find your place yet?" I told her my tale of woes, and she chided me lovingly: "Oh ye of little faith! Come on, girl, you can do this." I hung up the phone. *She's right. I can't give up on my dream just because the going is tough.* I sat cross-legged on the couch, plopped my dog in my lap, and meditated vigorously on my dream home before going off to work.

That afternoon, my real-estate agent called. "I think I've found something for you. It's not even on the market yet. It's a little far, but I think you'll like it."

As we drove into the hills of Malibu, my heart sank. *Oh, no, not another house all by itself way out in the back of beyond.*

My real-estate agent peered at a sign. "Ah, I think this is the street." And she proceeded to drive up, and up and up, one hairpin turn after another, until she rounded that last corner, drove down a dirt driveway, stopped the car . . . and I fell in love. To my left, seen from the top of a hill, was the most splendid 180-degree view of the ocean. To my right stood a delightful two-story Cape Cod-style house in obvious need of considerable repair and, all around me, an unblemished state park.

"A fixer-upper," my real-estate agent said. "I didn't think you'd mind."

Mind? I was in heaven.

As I walked through the house, I watched my dream home—everything I had written down about it more than two years ago—came to life: floor-to-ceiling windows letting in the light, large airy rooms (even a loft!), and a backyard big enough for lots of pets.

I have since attracted many wonderful people, situations, and things into my life with appreciation. I am profoundly grateful for all of them. But none will ever have the place in my heart of this first incredible manifestation—the joyous proof of the power of loving intent, the power of appreciation.

Noelle Nelson

LIFE LESSON #4:
PUTTING ACTIONS TO YOUR INTENTIONS

Do you remember your childhood dreams of career choices, the man or woman of your dreams, or the prized sports car? Did you replace them with new dreams as you got older, like most people do? Have you attained your dreams? If not, why?

The saying, "We are the creators of our own destiny," is right on the mark! We spend a great deal of time thinking about what we want—what we want to be when we grow up, the type of lifestyle we would like to lead, the location and type of home we would like to own—but so many of these dreams do not come to fruition. Why? Because they are often just yearnings, hopes, or the proverbial brass ring. But they need not be. You can actually attain the things you have always wished for, but you need more than a vague idea of what is truly desired. You need to deliberately pursue your goal to create your reality.

Dreams and aspirations are kind of like seeds in a garden. Would you just plant seeds and leave them to fend for themselves, expecting them to grow into the desired fruit, vegetable, or flower? Of course not. Without water to stay quenched, fertilizer for growth, and regular weeding, your seeds would not thrive at all. In fact, they would just wither away. That is exactly what can happen to your dreams.

They will never flourish without thought, attention, and energy. Deliberate attention is needed. It is the process of putting action to your intentions that will help manifest your dreams.

Exercise

If your dreams have not yet become a reality, take some time to reflect on the reasons why. Ask yourself if there was something that you could have done to help them along. If the answer is yes, then you have a starting point for action.

In your Prosperity Journal, assemble a plan for how you are going to achieve your dreams. Action takes courage. The Universe recognizes courage as an acknowledgement that you are ready to handle the next step, whatever that next step may be. If you keep working toward your dreams and aspirations, you will achieve them.

Use action as the catalyst and watch what begins to manifest. You won't be surprised. After all, you made it become reality.

Life Lesson #5
Inner Guidance Is Always with You

We are not human beings having a
spiritual experience, but spiritual beings
having a human experience.

Pierre Teilhard de Chardin

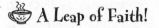 A Leap of Faith!

Sometimes, simply by sitting,
the soul collects wisdom.

ZEN PROVERB

A dozen years ago, I had a transformative encounter with what I call "divine energy" that changed me forever! Although others thought I was extremely fortunate and had a brilliant career, I felt nothing. That night as I sat and contemplated suicide once again, I suddenly realized that I wanted to make a difference in people's lives—to do something lasting and worthwhile.

In that one amazing moment, I knew my life purpose. I saw it outlined along with insights into my highest probable path. Immediately, my doubts tried to erase the vision by reminding me that I had no idea how to start over. That is when the most amazing awareness swept over me . . . Somehow, I had activated the ability to communicate directly with my Spiritual Source! Using this marvelous two-way communication, I started cleaning up the mess I had made of my life and set out to build a wonderful and more fulfilling life.

I began to pray and meditate—whenever and wherever—for any length of time. New-to-me methods and processes were downloaded to me empathically. I tested these thoughts rigorously, and they always produced tangible, practical results that ultimately created the framework of my present work as a spiritual coach. I was constantly provided with wisdom on how to live life to the fullest. No, I do not have special, arcane powers, but yes, we all have the ability to activate divine energy. I know because I have helped many others replicate my findings, too. Every day, I see its powerful ripple effect in all of our lives!

Peace on Earth will emerge from our deepest levels of sharing and caring about what we all choose to do and be, here and now, not from the superficial roles we assume in everyday life. Facades conceal our spiritual being. We need to recognize and honor the spiritual being that is the authentic you and me. That is why I am sharing my story with you.

I could say that after my initial mystical encounter, I ran out and immediately became a spiritual coach, but it did not happen that way. After my spiritual healing, I jumped headfirst into the study of spiritual, metaphysical, and healing philosophies, and became convinced that I was not the only one seeking a new life. This search made me even more determined to heal my life and create a better future that would produce everything I needed or even wanted.

Healing and prosperity are the same to me—a progressive process. I discovered that *by chance* I could easily find books with the answers I sought or *by chance* meet people who would immediately help me. Using my own two-way communication with the divine more and more, I *received* immediate in-depth answers to my most pressing problems! Suggestions, affirmations, exercises, plus what I called "divine prescriptions," came easily to me whenever I prayed. Each time, I trusted and implemented these *prescriptions*, my life changed. I began sharing them with others until they, too, saw their lives improve!

My husband and I had been trying for several years to have a child, and at one point I remember praying about getting pregnant. The response was, "Let go of your need to have a baby." We then agreed that if we never had a child, we would still be happy. We acknowledged that our happiness did not hinge on having children, and that if we did not have any, we would find other outlets for our parental love with nieces and nephews. One month later, I was pregnant!

When I was eight months pregnant, I remember writing in my journal, "What am I going to do when the baby is born since I want to serve God always? How can I do that and still make a good living?" I had asked this before and not received any specific answer. The now-familiar sensation that I get when on the receiving end of this two-way spiritual communication process began, and a flood of words poured through my pen onto the paper. "This would be a good time to open a coaching practice. Call it *A Choice for Joy!* Name your baby Joy, dedicate your coaching work to the Holy Spirit . . . and trust!" I remember staring at the paper thinking that this had to be a fantasy.

The next day, my mentor and teacher, Ruth Lee, handed me a magazine to read. She gave no instructions other than that it contained what I needed to know, and to read it cover-to-cover if necessary. Upon opening the magazine, I felt goose bumps and shivers unrelated to my advanced pregnancy. Tears streamed down my face as I read a headline: "Create a Life of Your Dreams—Be a Coach!" I *just knew* this was how I would create a better life—one of prosperity and divine inspiration! The article explained in detail the profession of coaching, a new idea at the time.

Amazed to read about what I had previously *received* through journaling my Divine Guidance System, I nevertheless struggled to believe that coaching others could be my career, too. The author listed organizations that offered training and mentioned a virtual university where you could take classes via phone, which was perfect for a mother with a newborn.

With joyful expectation, I wrote in my Journal: "Is this in my highest good to do this?" Struggling to write down the answer fast enough, I saw: "This is a good option. They will teach you the mechanics of creating a business, but *we* say you will go to this organization for reasons having nothing to do with the organization." I found that puzzling, but before fear could overcome me, I had a flashback to the night I had been healed. I remembered hearing, "One of your highest probable paths is to work with Workers of the Light . . . to help them release ego-concerns and connect with inner guidance, and *trust!*"

With a deep sense of *just knowing* that this would be my next step, I imagined how I would explain to my husband that I would not be going back to my executive position and would lose my high salary. When I told him *what I got* in my two-way communication, he smiled and said, "So, you're finally ready to commit to doing what you love? It's about time!"

At that moment, I knew something significant had changed within me, but would I allow myself to totally trust my spiritual guidance? What lay in store for me if I did? All I can say now is that it made no rational or logical sense to do it then, but I *knew* it was right! Never before had I had such a powerful inner knowing. It was exhilarating and scary at the same time, but I felt total peace. That inner power catapulted me into an incredible life that has surpassed my previous dreams—a life of love, joy, and prosperity. It is a life dedicated to serving and helping others awaken that same power within themselves! You cannot discover this work in a linear way. It has to come to your mind from your Spiritual Source!

Sharon Wilson

LIFE LESSON #5:
INNER GUIDANCE IS ALWAYS WITH YOU

We each have an inner guide, the voice that has the right answer but is sometimes overlooked. Our inner guides are always with us, but often muted. Later, when it is realized that the voice, intuition, or instinct should have been heeded, you may feel it's too late to correct the initial decision. But we are at choice at every moment! Sounds a little hard to believe, right? Who would choose to have a marriage dissolve, or a career end? But a little investigation will often uncover a *feeling* that this person is not exactly what was desired, but may be close enough. Or the job paid very well, so even if some of the tasks were not in alignment with the idea of the ideal job, it was worth it. In essence, choices were actually made to gag one's inner guide and roll with the situation.

How many times have you thought, *Man, if I had only listened to my instincts!* That was your inner guide telling you which way to proceed, and it was ignored. Do you know what is the largest population of inner-guide listeners? Children. That's one of the reasons they tend to get into so much trouble with adults—they do what their inner guide advises without thought to consequence or feelings. Their one goal is to do what they believe will make them happy at any given point in time, and they do. Children do not realize that the world does not revolve around them, but they also have not been taught that it's their job to make and keep everyone happy (a true fallacy in today's society). If everyone accepted responsibility for their own happiness—a true possibility when listening to our inner guides—the world would be a much happier and harmonious place.

Remember that the ultimate goal in life is J-O-Y, and it is your responsibility to create it for yourself. But it cannot be done without focus, intent, and practice.

Exercise

Learn to quiet the conscious thinking of the mind for no more than fifteen minutes each day and allow your inner guide to come through. Here's how:

1. Focus on breathing, or the flicker of a candle, or use an audible word like "Om."
2. Once the mind is quieted, physical detachment will occur, and you will be in a state of "allowing." This is when your inner being will take over. You may feel an involuntary movement in your body, like just before you're falling asleep and your foot moves, or you feel as if you're falling—this is the state where energies are in alignment.
3. Determine your path for allowing alignment energies to come through. It could be through blocks of thought, writing, a voice, or some other manner.

Everyone has the ability to hear their inner voice. The key is to find the time to make it happen and not censor what is coming through. Be consistent, and a mere thirty days is all it should take to get into the swing of things. Simply learn to relax, allow, and receive. Your happiness depends on it.

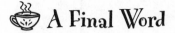 A Final Word

To accomplish great things, we must not only act,
but also dream; not only plan, but also believe.

ANATOLE FRANCE

It's never lack of money, time, or any other circumstance that prevents you from having what you want. It's about you deciding and believing you can have what you desire. It's an illusion to think otherwise. Remember that using the Law of Attraction in your life is a work in progress. We want you to wake up every day excited about your plans, with as much money as you desire rolling in, and all of your relationships filling you up. As you proceed, we know you have the power to be completely relaxed and at ease because the only actions you will be taking from now on are those that come from inspiration and joy.

Make life a game and keep it light! It's okay if you don't get it right every time. Keep looking for ways to enjoy the journey. Be willing to ask for what you want. Be willing to focus on what you want. As you do, you will become masterful at creating the best vision for your life that you can possibly imagine.

Our wish for you is to be happy, healthy, wealthy, vital, and alive; to live a life of freedom, joy, and prosperity; to know your worth and value in this world; and to allow yourself to bask in the love that surrounds you.

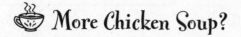

More Chicken Soup?

Many of the stories you have read in this book were submitted by readers like you who had read earlier Chicken Soup for the Soul books. We publish many Chicken Soup for the Soul books every year. We invite you to contribute a story to one of these future volumes.

Stories may be up to 1,200 words and must uplift or inspire.

To obtain a copy of our submission guidelines and a listing of upcoming Chicken Soup books, please write, fax, or check our website.

Please send your submissions to:

Chicken Soup for the Soul
P.O. Box 30880
Santa Barbara, CA 93130
fax: 805-563-2945
website: www.chickensoup.com

Just send a copy of your stories and other pieces to the above address. We will be sure that both you and the author are credited for your submission.

For information about speaking engagements, other books, audiotapes, workshops, and training programs, please contact any of our authors directly.

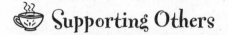
Supporting Others

In the spirit of supporting others, a portion of the proceeds from *Life Lessons for Mastering the Law of Attraction* will be donated to the **Peace Pedalers Relief Fund**.

The Peace Pedalers Relief Fund was started to give spontaneous and planned aid to families, individuals, and projects in need of financial support. The current and future projects of the Peace Pedalers Relief Fund include:

1) **Pedal Proud Campaign:** This ongoing project was started by part-time Peace Pedaler, Vanessa Lurie. In this campaign, they have already raised enough money to donate 100 bikes to South Africans to help assist in alleviating poverty, and increasing health and happiness. Bicycles are an excellent alternative to buses, taxis, and walking, which many Africans currently use as their method of transport. Bicycles allow them to save money and time to contribute more to their household needs and alleviate poverty.

2) **Spokes for Hope:** This is a new project where Peace Pedalers will partner with Novartis and The Global Fund to raise funds and awareness to fight AIDS, tuberculosis, and malaria. With support from Novartis, they will be pedaling hundreds of the malaria treatment Coartem to cure children and adults in clinics and villages along their route. We invite people to investigate The Global Fund and the many initiatives worldwide such as Product Red that support the vision to alleviate unnecessary suffering in Africa.

3) **School Supply Delivery:** Many children around the world do not have pencils, pens, or notepads. They have a huge desire to learn, but need tools to do so. Peace Pedalers has delivered hundreds of packages of school supplies to orphans and

children in need along their journey and will continue to do this as funds permit.

4) **Orphanage Visits:** Peace Pedalers has visited dozens of orphanages to put smiles on the faces of children and let them know they are loved and respected. They give presentations and show photos and videos to inspire them to dream big and believe in themselves. They often bring gifts of toys and school supplies, and always give out stickers and bracelets as a reminder that people do care.

5) **Grassroots Aid:** As Peace Pedaler founder, Jamie Bianchini, pedals north toward Morocco, he will no doubt run into people who need aid immediately and directly. Whether a child in need of medical attention, a community in need of a new water pump, or a hospital in need of supplies—we hope to have the Relief Fund stocked up enough to be able to deliver this much-needed grassroots aid.

6) **PRAKsters:** PRAKsters is an acronym for Practice Random Acts of Kindness. Jamie has a special PRAKster costume and will be out spreading love and kindness, and documenting the faces and responses of the recipients in a sneaky, stealth segment of his filming efforts. This project is all about looking for ways to put smiles on the faces of those in need. Whether it's delivering a basket of food to a hungry family, school supplies to a group of kids, or medical supplies to a clinic, this fun project is going to be a blast! We'll use funds from the Peace Pedalers Relief Fund when necessary, but usually it will be paid for by founder Jamie Bianchini.

For information on programs, services, and events, please contact:

Peace Pedalers World HQ
Attn: Carol "Mamacita" Fabian
2029 Oliver Avenue
San Diego, CA 92109
Phone: 1-858-274-1878 • mobile: 1-619-990-4989
E-mail: mamacitas@peacepedalers.com

Who Is Jack Canfield?

Jack Canfield is the cocreator and editor of the Chicken Soup for the Soul series, which *Time* magazine has called "the publishing phenomenon of the decade." The series includes more than 140 titles with over 100 million copies in print in forty-seven languages. Jack is also the coauthor of eight other best-selling books, including *The Success Principles™: How to Get from Where You Are to Where You Want to Be, Dare to Win, The Aladdin Factor, You've Got to Read This Book,* and *The Power of Focus: How to Hit Your Business, Personal and Financial Targets with Absolute Certainty.*

Jack has recently developed a telephone coaching program and an online coaching program based on his most recent book, *The Success Principles.* He also offers a seven-day Breakthrough to Success seminar every summer, which attracts 400 people from about fifteen countries around the world.

Jack is the CEO of Chicken Soup for the Soul Enterprises and the Canfield Training Group in Santa Barbara, California, and is founder of the Foundation for Self-Esteem in Culver City, California. He has conducted intensive personal and professional development seminars on the principles of success for more than a million people in twenty-nine countries around the world. Jack is a dynamic keynote speaker, and he has spoken to hundreds of thousands of others at more than 1,000 corporations, universities, professional conferences, and conventions and has been seen by millions more on national television shows such as *Oprah, Montel, The Today Show, Larry King Live, Fox and Friends, Inside Edition, Hard Copy,* CNN's *Talk Back Live, 20/20, Eye to Eye,* and the *NBC Nightly News* and the *CBS Evening News.* Jack was also a featured teacher in the hit movie *The Secret.*

Jack is the recipient of many awards and honors, including three honorary doctorates and a Guinness World Records Certificate for having seven books from the Chicken Soup for the Soul series appearing on the *New York Times* bestseller list on May 24, 1998.

To write to Jack or for inquiries about Jack as a speaker, his coaching programs, trainings, or seminars, use the following contact information:

Jack Canfield
The Canfield Companies
P.O. Box 30880 • Santa Barbara, CA 93130
Phone: 805-563-2935 • Fax: 805-563-2945
E-mail: info4jack@jackcanfield.com
www.jackcanfield.com

Who Is Mark Victor Hansen?

In the area of human potential, no one is more respected than Mark Victor Hansen. For more than thirty years, Mark has focused solely on helping people from all walks of life reshape their personal vision of what's possible. His powerful messages of possibility, opportunity, and action have created powerful change in thousands of organizations and millions of individuals worldwide.

He is a sought-after keynote speaker, bestselling author, and marketing maven. Mark's credentials include a lifetime of entrepreneurial success and an extensive academic background. He is a prolific writer with many bestselling books, such as *The One Minute Millionaire, Cracking the Millionaire Code, How to Make the Rest of Your Life the Best of Your Life, The Power of Focus, The Aladdin Factor,* and *Dare to Win,* in addition to the Chicken Soup for the Soul series. Mark has made a profound influence through his library of audios, videos, and articles in the areas of big thinking, sales achievement, wealth building, publishing success, and personal and professional development.

Mark is the founder of the MEGA Seminar Series. MEGA Book Marketing University and Building Your MEGA Speaking Empire are annual conferences where Mark coaches and teaches new and aspiring authors, speakers, and experts on building lucrative publishing and speaking careers. Other MEGA events include MEGA Info-Marketing and My MEGA Life.

As a philanthropist and humanitarian, Mark works tirelessly for organizations such as Habitat for Humanity, American Red Cross, March of Dimes, Childhelp USA, and many others. He is the recipient of numerous awards that honor his entrepreneurial spirit, philanthropic heart, and business acumen. He is a lifetime member of the Horatio Alger Association of Distinguished Americans, an organization that honored Mark with the prestigious Horatio Alger Award for his extraordinary life achievements.

Mark Victor Hansen is an enthusiastic crusader of what's possible and is driven to make the world a better place.

Mark Victor Hansen & Associates, Inc.
P.O. Box 7665 • Newport Beach, CA 92658
Phone: 949-764-2640 • Fax: 949-722-6912
www.markvictorhansen.com

Who Is Jeanna Gabellini?

Jeanna Gabellini, CPCC, is a master coach, speaker, and author of several programs and books including *The Art of Practice, Speed Dial the Universe, Mind Games, The Prosperity Game Home Study Course, The Magnetizing Money Course*, and *Financial Fortune*. She has instructed tens of thousands in person, on the radio, and in teleconferences on how to get exactly what they want by using the Laws of Attraction.

Jeanna is regularly featured the media and is a recognized authority on the Laws of Attraction. As co-host of *The Jeanna and Eva Show*, she has interviewed some of the most successful motivational experts today.

In 1998, she was one of the first coaches in the world—and the youngest—to receive the designation of Master Certified Coach by the International Coach Federation. Jeanna has served on the board of both the Personal & Professional Coaching Association and the International Coach Federation.

She is known as the Extreme Abundance Coach, bringing both strategy and outrageous laughs to business teams and individuals. She teaches her clients how to go big with a ton of fun!

Jeanna delivers keynote addresses, workshops, seminars and teleconferences both nationally and internationally. For more information about Jeanna's books, programs, and coaching or to schedule her for a presentation, please contact:

MasterPeace Coaching & Training
Phone: 707-747-0447
Email: Jeanna@MasterPeaceCoaching.com
Website: www.MasterPeaceCoaching.com

Who Is Eva Gregory?

Eva Gregory, CPCC, is a master coach, speaker, and author of several programs and books, including *The Feel Good Guide to Prosperity, The Prosperity Game Home Study Course*, and *Law of Attraction Hot Topics*. She has instructed thousands of individuals on how to create a life by design using the Law of Attraction.

Eva is regularly featured on radio and in the media and is a recognized authority on the Law of Attraction. As cohost of *The Jeanna and Eva Show*, she has interviewed some of the most successful inspirational experts today.

She is an Executive Producer for a positive music label, Googol Press.

Eva empowers her clients in their business and personal lives. Her unwavering belief is that all of us have the power to change anything in our lives and design it purposefully.

Her business background includes over twenty years in finance and operations and marketing with a Fortune 100 corporation; as marketing executive of a software firm; and Chief Fun Officer of Leading Edge Coaching & Training.

She is a member of National Association of Female Executives, Networking Women International, Women's E-Commerce Association, Association of Coaching & Consulting Professionals and International Association of Coaches.

Her most popular programs are her Bigger Impact Law of Attraction Certification Program for coaches and her Leading Edge Success Club membership site.

Eva delivers keynote addresses, workshops, seminars, and teleconferences nationally and internationally. For more information about Eva's books, programs, and other services or to schedule her for a presentation, please contact:

Leading Edge Coaching & Training
P O Box 99656
Emeryville, CA 94662
Phone: 510-597-0687 • Fax: 510-588-5477
FREE resources online at: www.EvaGregory.com

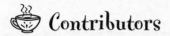 **Contributors**

Licia Berry is a teacher, artist, and writer. Currently writing her book, *Road Trip to the Heart* (a family love story), she chronicles the epic journey her family of four made to recover their lost connection. She can be contacted by e-mail at licia@liciaberry.com or through their family website at www.berrytrip.us.

Christine Brooks received her Bachelor of Arts, with honors, from Western New England College. Christine enjoys traveling to write and surf. She has completed her first book, *Signs from the Road*, and her second, *A Voice to Be Heard*, is due out in early 2008. Please e-mail her at chris@fourleafclover.us.

Jim Bunch is a widely respected coach, speaker, and entrepreneur whose mission is to inspire happiness, health, and wealth worldwide through transformational coaching programs, seminars, and products. To stay connected to the latest information in creating Happy, Healthy, and Wealthy lives, be sure to visit us at www.JimBunch.com or call 888-335-3880 for more information.

Kathleen Carroll, author of CDs with songs and stories, and books on science education and field trips, presents in the United States and abroad on accelerated learning, authentic assessment, science education, and teaching the whole person.

Sonia Choquette is a world-renowned revolutionary intuitive, healer, and spirited teacher. A masterful visionary committed to activating the highest vibrational and intuitive potential in all, she is the best-selling author of eight books: *The Psychic Pathway, Your Heart's Desire, The Intuitive Spark, True Balance, The Diary of a Psychic, Trust Your Vibes,* and numerous audio editions. She can be reached via email at sonia@soniachoquette.com.

Idelisa Cintron graduated from Chapman University and is the founder of www.LOA Connections.com, a global social community where believers of the Law of Attraction can come together. She lives in Southern California and loves spending time with her husband and three children, painting, writing, and following the Law of Attraction.

Patricia Daniels, a recognized authority on self-empowerment and self-healing, is an inspirational speaker, writer, life coach, and healer. She coaches business professionals, artists, and individuals from four countries. Patricia's ability to create unique improvisational games specific to her clients' and seminar participants' needs is awe-inspiring. Contact her through www.mission-empowerment.com.

Dr. John F. Demartini is an inspirational speaker, bestselling author, and consultant. He is the founder of The Demartini Human Research Foundation and the Concourse of Wisdom School, creator of The Breakthrough Experience and originator of The Demartini Method. For information, visit his website at www.drdemartini.com.

Terri Elders, LCSW, lives in prosperous semi-retirement on three and a half acres in northeast Washington, where she devotes her days to one husband (Ken Wilson), two dogs, three cats, and four part-time jobs, including freelance writing and editing. She can be reached at telders@hotmail.com.

David B. Ellis is a nationally known author, life coach, philanthropist, and workshop facilitator. Through his workshops and books he has helped over four million people create a more wonderful life. Dave has written seven books, including the best-selling college text in America. He is founder and president of The Brande Foundation.

Hayley Foster transformed herself from homemaker to professional speaker, author, trainer, and consultant using the Law of Attraction, among other skills. *Divided Loyalties: the career You Crave and the family You Love*, grew out of this transition. You can reach her via email at hayley@hayleyfoster.com or visit her website at www.hayleyfoster.com.

Barb Gau, MSW, LCSW, is a retired psychotherapist and Duke University faculty member. She loves teaching and sharing the LOA with her network marketing team. She lives in Chapel Hill, North Carolina (aka The Southern Part of Heaven), with her amazing husband, Larry, and Alaskan malamute, Teka. Her website is www.VibrantLivingCenter.com.

Rene Godefroy is a performance and change expert. He is the author of *Kick Your Excuses Good-Bye*. Rene inspires audiences to go an extra mile in everything and be more open to change. For more information on how to book Rene to boost morale in your organization, visit www.GoAnExtraMile.com.

Ruben Gonzalez competed in three Olympics in three different decades. Ruben is an award-winning keynote speaker, the author of *The Courage to Succeed*, and co-star of the movie, *Pass It On*. Visit www.OlympicMotivation.com for Ruben's free success course.

Since age thirteen, **Amy Scott Grant** has captivated audiences of all ages with her razor-sharp wit, contagious enthusiasm, and bold authenticity. With a gifted vision, a passion for transformation, and a no-nonsense demeanor, Amy is a powerful coach, author, speaker, and creator of NewSuccess.org, the ultimate success resource.

Catherine Ripley Greene, D.C., owns and directs Ripley Greene Chiropractic Wellness Center in Walpole, Massachusetts. Combining her experience as a practicing doctor with her intuitive gifts, she provides her clients with a unique healing experience.

Betty Healey, M.Ed., is a certified and licensed Strategic Attraction Coach and your travel guide for self-discovery. An award-winning author, Betty has published two books, *roadSIGNS: Travel Tips for Authentic Living* and *roadSIGNS2: Travel Tips to Higher Ground*. For more information about Betty and *roadSIGNS*, visit www.roadSIGNS.ca.

Jan Henrikson relishes abundance of all kinds in Tucson, Arizona. She is editor of *Eat by Choice, Not by Habit* by Sylvia Haskvitz (Puddle Dancer Press). Her next creative collaboration is a book with Tryshe Dhevney on healing with the sound of your voice (www.soundshifting.com). Contact her at jan@o-c-e-a-n.com.

Kristy Iris, MFA, is the founder of Fizom, which helps you create an environment that supports success. Discover how you can use the Law of Attraction in your home or business by visiting www.fizom.com and signing up for free Fiztips today!

Charles M. Marcus is the president of the Empowerment International Group, Inc., based in Toronto, Canada. He is a much sought-after motivational speaker, success strategist, and bestselling author. For further information about Charles, please visit his website at www.cmarcus.com. E-mail him at charles@cmarcus.com or call toll-free at 800-837-0629.

Jeannette Maw resides in Salt Lake City, Utah, with her three dogs with whom she loves to hike and camp. In addition to volunteering in animal rescue, Jeannette is founder of Good Vibe Coaching, which allows her to share her passion for deliberate creation. Visit www.goodvibecoach.com or e-mail jmaw@goodvibecoach.com.

Noelle C. Nelson, Ph.D., internationally acclaimed psychologist, author, and speaker, focuses on how we can accomplish great things at work, at home and in love using the power of appreciation. Author of ten books, her latest is *"Men Are Wonderful"* (working title); Free Press, January 2009. Website: www.noellenelson.com.

Maureen O'Shaughnessy, author of *My Naked Journey: A Reiki Master's Quest to Live Authentically* (available through Amazon.com), is a speaker and seminar facilitator who has lived in Hawaii for more than twenty-five years. Maureen travels frequently, speaking on numerous radio and television shows, and offering seminars throughout North America. Visit www.Reiki-Hawaii.com.

Holleay T. Parcker is a licensed North Carolina real-estate broker and owner of Spinnaker Realty LLC. Holleay is writing a light-hearted and inspiring book that she intends to serve as a roadmap to success in real estate. E-mail Holleay at holleay@OuterBanksRealEstateTips.com or call her toll-free at 877-207-1617.

Mark Parisi's "off the mark" comic, syndicated since 1987, is distributed by United Media. Mark's humor also graces greeting cards, T-shirts, calendars, magazines, newsletters and books. Check out: offthemark.com. Lynn is his wife/business partner. Their daughter, Jen, contributes with inspiration (as do three cats).

Wanda Peyton is the CEO of _____ nter in Fontana California and the founder _____ Peyton Motivational Seminars. She is an emotional energy management coach and motivational speaker, sharing her personal experiences in living the law of attraction. Her contact information is wanda@shewhowhispers.com www.shewhowhispers.com.

Patrick Snow is the bestselling author of *Creating Your Own Destiny*, which has sold more than 100,000 copies worldwide and has been featured in a cover story in *USA Today*. He is also a keynote speaker and publishing coach. He can be reached at 800-951-7721 or www.CreateYourOwnDestiny.com.

Allison Sodha is the owner of Sodha Travel, a company that specializes in travel to India. She received her B.A. in Religious Studies with an emphasis in Hinduism and has written freelance articles for *Little India* magazine. To contact Allison, please visit www.sodhatravel.com or e-mail her at Allison@sodhatravel.com.

Jan H. Stringer resides in Santa Fe, New Mexico, and is co-founder of PerfectCustomers, Inc. and SACAT Corporation. Her proprietary method called Strategic _____ *Attracting Perfect C* _____ *ing Perfect:* Wealth, _____ website at www.perf

Carol Tuttle _____ n the areas of Energ _____ *membering Wholenes* _____ learn more about Ca

Dr. Joe Vita _____ bestsellers *The Attra* _____ any more, including _____ com.

Jillian Coleman Wheeler is author of *The Other Secrets: Beyond the Law of Attraction*, and co-author, with Joe Vitale, of *Your Internet Cash Machine: The Insiders Guide to Making Big Money, Fast*. Read more about Jillian and her work at www.DrJillian.com, www.GrantMeRich.com, www.YourInternetCashMachine.com, and www.NewAmerican LandRush.com.

Sharon Wilson is the founder and "chief inspiration officer" at the Coaching from Spirit Institute. Her programs serve individuals, businesses, mega-corporations, and life-development coaches to activate their highest possibilites. She is a Certified Spiritual Counselor and co-author of three books. Go to www.coachingfromspirit.com for free resources.